"*Missional* may well be the best yet from author Alan Roxburgh as he prophetically reclaims the Newbigin engagement of gospel and culture as the key to rediscovering what it really means to be church. This engagement is compellingly framed in theological terms from the Luke-Acts texts as readers are deeply challenged and creatively invited to 'join God in their neighborhoods.' A must-read for anyone who take seriously the challenge and opportunity facing the church in the West in light of it having lost home field advantage."

—**Craig Van Gelder**, PhD, Professor of Congregational Mission, Luther Seminary, Saint Paul, MN

"I've read Al Roxburgh over the years and, taking nothing away from his previous work, this is Roxburgh's finest to date. His take on Luke 10 is compelling. Filled with stories and theological precision, this book takes us to new places for the future of Christ's church in North America. It is sure to be a tour de force for the missional conversation. I am not being excessive when I say this book is brilliant."

—**David Fitch**, B. R. Lindner Professor of Evangelical Theology, Northern Seminary; author, *The End of Evangelicalism?*

"Many have undertaken to set down an orderly account of things called 'missional,' but Roxburgh deconstructs our modern strategic orderliness, claims we often ask the wrong questions, and lures us into Luke's narratives. Roxburgh posits that our 'language house,' our whole imagination about what God is up to and how we might participate, needs to be upended through some rather odd activities like listening to neighbors and rehearing some biblical narratives."

—**Rev. Mark Lau Branson**, EdD, Homer Goddard Associate Professor of Ministry of the Laity, Fuller Theological Seminary

"The term 'missional' is in serious danger of becoming all things to all people and thereby signifying nothing. In this book, Alan Roxburgh offers an important corrective to this situation by providing a concrete, practical, and theologically sophisticated conception of the term in conjunction with a fresh imagination around the idea of joining God in the neighborhood for the sake of the world. This is the best book yet from one of the leading voices in the missional conversation."

—**John R. Franke**, Theologian in Residence, First Presbyterian Church of Allentown; general coordinator, the Gospel and Our Culture Network

"Roxburgh daringly puts the church in its place . . . literally. *Missional* invites us to relocate the center of missional life from churches to our places and neighborhoods. Drawing on a lifetime of missional practice and study, Roxburgh brings together missional theology with real world stories of missional practitioners. A must-read for any community seeking to live even more missionally."

—**Dwight J. Friesen**, Associate Professor of Practical Theology, Mars Hill Graduate School, Seattle; author, *Thy Kingdom Connected*; co-author, *Routes and Radishes*

"Many books are worth reading but few worth absorbing. This book falls into the latter category, and if you allow it to, it will take you into a new world and give you eyes to see what God is doing all around you. It will put 'mission' into your understanding of 'missional.'"

—**M. Scott Boren**, pastor; author, *Missional Small Groups*

"*Missional* is a must-read for pastors and church leaders who want a biblical framework and practical process for being the church in our time, not just doing church in the cookie-cutter style of other churches. Because *Missional* begins by asking the right questions and not giving the right answers, we are drawn into our own conversations about what it means to be sent, to move back into our neighborhoods, and to spark the missional imaginations of our church members for the sake of the gospel."

—**Mike McClenahan**, senior pastor, Solana Beach Presbyterian Church, board member, Presbyterian Global Fellowship and Amor Ministries

MISSION IN WESTERN CULTURE PROJECT

Also in the Allelon Missional Series

ChurchMorph
Eddie Gibbs

Introducing the Missional Church
Alan J. Roxburgh and M. Scott Boren

Missional Small Groups
M. Scott Boren

Missional
Alan J. Roxburgh

ALLELON MISSIONAL SERIES

MISSIONAL

JOINING GOD IN THE NEIGHBORHOOD

ALAN J. ROXBURGH

BakerBooks

a division of Baker Publishing Group
Grand Rapids, Michigan

© 2011 by Allelon

Published by Baker Books
a division of Baker Publishing Group
P.O. Box 6287, Grand Rapids, MI 49516-6287
www.bakerbooks.com

Printed in the United States of America

Library of Congress Cataloging-in-Publication Data
Roxburgh, Alan J.
      Missional : joining God in the neighborhood / Alan J. Roxburgh.
         p.   cm. — (Allelon missional series)
      Includes bibliographical references (p.   ).
      ISBN 978-0-8010-7231-4 (pbk.)
      1. Mission of the church. 2. Missions—Theory. 3. Bible. N.T. Luke X, 1–12—Criticism, interpretation, etc. I. Title.
BV601.8.R689 2010
266.001—dc22   2010041220

11   12   13   14   15   16   17   7 6 5 4 3 2 1

Contents

Series Preface

Allelon is a network of missional church leaders, schools, and para-church organizations that envisions, inspires, engages, resources, trains, and educates leaders for the church and its mission in our culture. Said simply, together we are a movement of missional leaders.

We have a particular burden for people involved in new forms of missional communities (sometimes called "emerging"), people starting new congregations within denominational systems, and people in existing congregations who are working toward missional identity and engagement. Our desire is to encourage, support, coach, and offer companionship for missional leaders as they discern new models of church capable of sustaining a living and faithful witness to the gospel in our contemporary world.

The word *allelon* is a common but overlooked Greek word that is reciprocal in nature. In the New Testament it is most often translated "one another." Christian faith is not an individual matter. Everything in the life of the church is done *allelon* for the sake of the world. A Christian community is shaped by the *allelon* sayings in the Scriptures, a few of which include love one another, pursue one another's good, and build up one another.

As a network of leaders who work with one another, leaders from multiple continents are currently working on a multiyear research project called Mission in Globalizing Culture. Through this project they are asking questions about the formation of leaders in a radically changing context and the demands of a multinarrative world.

Allelon also collaborates with the Roxburgh Missional Network in its research projects and in providing on-the-ground tools for leaders at all levels of church life. Through its website and consulting and training processes it is furthering the missional conversation in many parts of the world.

In addition, Allelon has partnered with Baker Books and Baker Academic to produce resources that equip the church with the best thinking and practices on missional life. The book you now hold is one of those pieces that contribute to the missional conversation and its practical outworking in local churches. I (Alan) have known and worked off and on with Scott for more than fifteen years. In that time, he has passionately sought ways in which small groups can be effective structures for the formation of people to be what Lesslie Newbigin described as a sign, foretaste, and witness of God's future in Jesus Christ. I have watched Scott wrestle with the big issues around forming missional groups at the heart of local churches. He understands how most small groups have been turned into little more than experiences for individuals and fail to participate in God's great purposes in creation. Scott has worked in local churches to produce something very different. This is not a "how-to-guide" as much as a handbook for leaders wondering how to empower and energize a community seeking to witness to the kingdom in the midst of their lives.

Mark Priddy and Al Roxburgh

Introduction

Welcome to an Unthinkable World

The argument of this book is that we have entered a world for which the churches of North America are woefully unprepared. These churches are, in fact, seeking to address this new, unthinkable world with strategies shaped in the twentieth century and with some of the deepest convictions of modernity.[1]

Further, I will argue that in this unthinkable space we do not need to jump into some new, so-called postmodern idealism. Instead we must return to some of the most basic imaginations given to us in the New Testament. We will look at the experience of Jesus's sending out the seventy disciples into the towns and villages of Galilee (Luke 10:1–12) and discover clues given there about how to navigate in an unthinkable world.[2]

The temptation, almost as if it is a default built into our DNA, is either to imagine we can solve the challenges of an unthinkable world using the categories of leadership that have worked for us in the past or to believe the new gurus of the church who suggest we need to abandon all the things we've done and buy their new visions of how things ought to be. As we begin this journey, some examples of how we tend to engage an unthinkable time will help guide our conversation.

A Lesson from History

In the mid-1930s the War to End All Wars had been over for more than a decade and much had changed since the Armistice in 1919. Following the Versailles Treaty came reparations, the disarmament of Germany, the formation of the League of Nations (to ensure that war could never break out again in the world), the redrawing of the map of Europe (to say nothing about the maps of the rest of the world, especially the Middle East where in this period so much of our current, indecipherable, international challenges began to emerge) to satisfy the victors, and a recognition that a new Europe was emerging in the east, and with it a most potent enemy—Soviet Communism.

Indeed, the Europe of the late thirties was either enthralled with or threatened by the new Communist movement growing under Stalin and then Lenin in Russia. For example, the American heiress Beatrice Webb moved to Paris, then London, where she and her husband set up salons for the avant-garde who regarded the new Soviet Russia as the vanguard of the future. Others viewed Soviet Russia as an emerging and terrifying threat to the free world.

Russia held the attention of leaders in Britain and France. Though the other European extreme, Fascism, was growing in a resurgent Germany, and Spain was embroiled in civil war, the biggest concern by far was Russia and Marxism. In this interwar period, while Germany rearmed and few attended to the voices that cried out about the destruction under Stalin, most of Europe was anxious about Stalin but wanted to placate him to win support against Germany.

Meanwhile, Germany was militarizing at an alarming rate. Its factories manufactured tanks at a breakneck pace. By 1938 France already had incontrovertible evidence that Germany was planning a massive tank assault. German military tacticians had written books outlining the details of such an attack along with maps showing the route the German Panzer movement would take through the forests of Belgium and deep into France. French spies had witnessed German tank divisions practicing these tactics in Poland and reported their findings to the French military. These spies, placed inside German military planning headquarters, had gathered enough information to confirm that the Belgian forests would be the attack route.

None of this information, however, affected French determination of what Germany would do. French generals had been shaped by the trauma of 1914–1919, when Germany came so close to defeating France and millions of brave French lives were lost in the trenches. They could not forget their own history. The result was that the French planning staff expected and prepared for a German attack across the eastern frontier and so they built the Maginot Line, a series of forts and defense systems designed to keep Germany at bay until the bulk of the French army could outflank them. France prepared on the basis of the last war; its leaders could not imagine any other scenario but an assault across the Maginot Line.

At the same time, Germany had its own memories of the Great War and its aftermath. The German imagination was shaped by humiliation and the conviction that its own military elite had betrayed the German people by making peace. In Hitler and much of the regular army lay a determination to right the wrongs of 1919 and return Germany to the glory of its past *geist* (spirit). Driven by this imagination, the German military chose to plan the unthinkable—a massive tank attack through the Belgian forests into France. They went on maneuvers, created innovative methods for moving between trees, and built tanks that could move quickly through forests.

When presented with intelligence concerning German plans, French military and political leadership chose to discount it and focus on the Maginot Line. Not able to imagine the unthinkable, they allowed the memories of the previous war to shape their plans for the next one. But the events of 1939 would show how disastrous France's long-established assumptions about warring with Germany really were. It was a different world, and they could not adequately address the crisis.

This dilemma of using outdated methods to meet a current challenge is now facing Christian life in the West.

Seeing Our Situation

A group of pastors were working together with a missional leadership-readiness report our organization had created, based on our 360 Discovery process they'd taken several weeks earlier.[3] One section of the report looks at a leader's capacity to engage the context in which his or her church is located—the neighborhoods and communities where members live and work.

I'll never forget the comment of one of the pastors. Lee, in his early forties, pastors a small church with a long history. He had been sitting silent for much of the morning but, when he spoke—quietly, pensively, and without fanfare—his words were like the live end of a high-voltage wire. A fissure seemed to open in the room and it couldn't be closed again.

He said, "I've just had an epiphany! Our church is across the road from a high school and every year at the time of football and basketball games or graduation, we put on events for the school. It's really nice, with food and entertainment and so on. Lots of people from the community come; kids and their parents turn up to enjoy what we provide. But it just struck me: we can put these events on forever, but these people aren't going to come and be a part of our church. And I have no idea what to do about it!"

Lee spoke without anger, accusation, or resignation. He simply saw the situation for what it was. An attractional church (a church where the primary energy is focused on how to get people to come to church) will not connect with growing numbers of people for whom church is nice to have around but is not integral to the structures or expectations of everyday life. It is still possible to attract Christians from other churches to better programs. For a lot of other people, however, their involvement ends after they have enjoyed the dinners and/or special events the church offers them. These folks aren't joining. A different kind of church is needed to meet the needs of people like this.

Disconnected

A call came from a young pastor down the valley from where I live in Vancouver. We needed to follow up on an earlier conversation, so we agreed to connect at Earl's restaurant, a hot spot in downtown Vancouver. When we got there, all kinds of young adults were crowded around tables with beer and food, engaged in loud, heated conversations.

The pastor brought along a friend who worked with young adults as a social worker and therapist. They had gone to the same seminary together a number of years before. In the course of our conversation, I asked the friend, who wore a turned-around baseball cap, where he was going to church. This elicited a familiar silence and momentary awkwardness. Finally, he said, "I don't go anywhere! It's not that I don't want to be part of a church community, but I just can't connect with what happens in those places anymore. I'll probably join a house church with some friends and see where that goes."

I wasn't surprised by this response. I've heard it over and over again from all kinds of people of all ages. I have friends who served effectively for years in Young Life; now in their early forties, they have checked out of church.

At a wedding reception I sat beside a woman in her fifties, an executive in a financial organization, who had been raised a Mennonite and attended church all her life. When I asked her that question, she looked at me with a pained expression and said she couldn't deal with the irrelevance of church any longer.

After forty years of leadership in all kinds of church contexts, I have never heard or felt such a level of disconnectedness with existing churches as I do now. What struck me was that the young social worker and older executive weren't angry or negative about Christian life. They weren't carrying on a diatribe against the church. This was something different—there was a longing to be part of something that called for a deep involvement in gospel living, but there was also a sadness because they sensed that, across a whole range of church systems, this involvement just couldn't be found.

The pastor and his friend told me about the seminary they'd attended. Each was in a graduating class of sixty to seventy people, all of whom were trained to enter what they called "the ministry." Ten years out, only one or two were actually practicing "ministry" as full-time leaders in churches. This is a stunning attrition rate for a conservative denomination rooted in an evangelical missions theology in North America.

I could tell story after story, and I suspect you could too, of people who have dropped out of church. Something is happening and it's not just generational. Christians are giving up on the church they have known. They feel adrift, having come to the conclusion that it's impossible to find a place to practice the Christian life, except in small house or simple churches that gather informally across the city. We have entered an unthinkable world where we need a different kind of church.

This book articulates what might be involved in rethinking Christian life in an unthinkable world. It comes out of my own wrestling with questions about what God might be about in our neighborhoods, cities, towns, and villages. It seeks to address questions about how we can faithfully engage during a time when so many of our churches have lost their capacity to engage the people in their communities.

PART I

THE CUL-DE-SAC OF OLD QUESTIONS

WHY WE HAVE TO STOP THINKING ABOUT THE CHURCH

1

Coral Reefs, Garage Sales, and Other Mind-Blowing Disturbances

Grappling with a New World

A friend of mine is a marine biologist. Tamara studies the oceans and the life that lies within them; more specifically, she studies how food chains interact with one another. Now teaching at Dalhousie University in Halifax, she's traveled the world, scuba diving in some of the most beautiful waters on this planet. When she was home in Vancouver a while back, my wife, Jane, and I had supper with her and her folks. As we ate, we could look out across the Georgia Strait to the San Juan Islands and beyond that to the mountains on Vancouver Island. We talked about the oceans, and I recalled a trip Jane and I took to northern Australia and the Whitsunday Islands in the Coral Sea. We went out to the Great Barrier Reef where I scuba dived for the first time in my life and thought I'd found the meaning of life (for a brief moment). We talked about the coral reefs around the world, and Tamara's comments about them still haunt me.

She said they are dying, all of them, and there is nothing anyone can do about it. Even if we started doing everything in our power to reverse global warming and global pollution, the factors were already in place for the destruction of these beautiful reefs with their collection of fish.

I recalled swimming among thousands of small, colored fish as they turned this way and that through clear water. Awed, I was stunned and silent. Now I realize I was in the midst of a delicate ecosystem that took billions of years to emerge and that was coming to an end. In less than a generation, it will all be swept away. What a startling thing to hear! I can still go to the reefs in Australia or the Caribbean and scuba dive amid their beauty. I can continue to swim among them as if nothing has changed, as if they will all still be there in the future. How do I get my head around the fact that in a generation they'll all be dead?

A Slow Death

The predicament of the coral reefs reminds me of the condition of the church today, but the forthcoming death of the reefs is more than just a metaphor. Our planet is dying, and we humans have had a lot to do with it. If we continue on this course, certain species will disappear. As the earth warms up, ice caps melt, weather becomes more extreme, and destructive patterns intensify. How do communities of God's people care for the earth and honor the creation as a gift?

I think about those dying reefs when people talk about successful "seeker" churches or the mega churches of North America. When I suggest that everything has to change, people argue that there are still methods and strategies to keep this church successful. Their implicit criticism comes through: Why are you so negative, always raising questions about the church and its future? It's as though people are swimming among the coral reefs, and from their perspective, everything looks fine—the reefs will last forever. They can't see what is happening before their eyes.

I can sense the processes of change gathering momentum all about us, and more than minor adjustments are needed. Up to this point the church has dealt with loss of place and identity in the community by trying out better marketing, offering a coffee bar on Sunday morning, providing a greater variety of options in terms of meeting personal taste in worship styles—introducing videos rather than sermons and candles where there had been none before—establishing strategic planning, creating a multisite ministry, and deciding all we have to do is turn our attention from the inside to the outside. All of that is window dressing, offering little to a world that is rapidly losing its way, perishing in the midst of a sea of change none of us can begin to understand. And we are silent, complicit in the plan to do more window dressing.

The list of issues confronting us is long and raises many hard questions about what it means to be the church in this time and what place the gospel has in all this swirling change. These are the questions that can't be put off. Yet our response to them is inadequate. Changing forms and establishing programs are not what is needed. These got us into this mess in the first place.

Church leaders in places as far-flung and different as North America, Europe, Australia, Korea, and southern Africa are recognizing that the church is now a lot like the Great Barrier Reef. We might have strategies for dressing it up to make it look more successful, but there is something wrong at the core that causes many to wonder if there is any possibility of transforming the church in its current forms. I found myself asking these questions shortly after I left pastoral leadership more than a decade ago.

Over the past twenty-five years much has been written about the need for the church to change; however, if we are to hear what God might be doing in the massively shifting contexts in which we live, we must move beyond conversations about the church, about how to make it work, and about patterns for success. I find most of these conversations are really seeking to restore the church to some imagined place in culture. I believe most of the questions we keep asking and most of the books on making the church work all point to the wrong solutions. In this book I propose that what I call "church questions," questions with a primary focus on the church, only misdirect us. At this point in our history, we need to be asking radically different questions: What is God up to in our neighborhoods and communities? How do we join with what God is doing in these places? Church questions are a subset of these far more important questions.

Coffee in False Creek on a Sunday Morning

One Sunday in early July, Jane and I drove across the Granville Bridge into the False Creek area where Aaron, our son, and Sonia, his wife, lived in a townhouse complex. Our grandson, Owen, was just two months old. On that beautiful sunny day, the complex at 8th Avenue and Granville was hosting a garage sale.

We arrived around midmorning after everything had already been neatly laid out on the sidewalk or gathered on separate tables in front of the townhouse entrance. Neighbors sat in chairs watching over their goods and chatting with one another; others stood around as potential buyers came early with their Starbucks in hand to see what bargains might be had. An array of bric-a-brac was available. Used Ikea kitchen chairs selling for five dollars each, a lot of hardly used wedding gifts, an assortment of used novels (mostly by Maeve Binchy and John Grisham) lined the sidewalk beside a huge, framed print of an Orca pod rising to the surface and blowing spouts of water into the air.

People were polite as they mingled to look at the cheap goods, engage in conversation, and discuss the assorted dogs they had in tow. And it was fascinating how normal it all seemed—this Sunday-morning milling about of neighbors and garage sale nomads.

Just a little farther down was Granville Island Market and then the False Creek developments along the water's edge with their dense communities of condos and townhouses, and the seawall walk around the whole inlet that went into Stanley Park. Every spot was alive with people. In this city on a Sunday morning, it was apparent that most folks were in coffee shops, running on the seawall, buying food at the market, or prowling tree-lined neighborhoods for garage sales and whatever else might be happening.

Apparently very few people were "in church" or even thought "church" had any relevance. Just up the street, not three blocks away, stood Holy Trinity Anglican. From attending this church from time to time, I knew there might have been seventy or so people there that morning but not many more. To the west another three or four blocks, hidden on a side street, was a little Presbyterian church with probably even fewer in attendance. In each there would be wonderful people; each would, in their own way, consider themselves providing a wonderful "family" experience for any who might venture into their "contemporary" or "traditional" services. I had learned that most of the people attending the Anglican church drive into the city from other areas. Perhaps the same is true for the Presbyterian congregation as well. It seemed obvious, however, that on this Sunday morning the real life of the city was not in the churches but outside at the garage sales, in the coffee shops, along the seawalls, and in the markets.

Of course this wasn't always so. And there still are places where you can see a different reality. Churches down the valley from Vancouver in Abbottsford, for example, as well as the suburban churches farther south of the city in places like Tsawassen are full. I've no doubt a few of the mega-wannabes could grow even bigger in the Pacific Northwest. Threads of the old story, when church was a central part of Canadian culture, remain. People will still drive great distances to find the church of which they want to be a part.

Not that long ago lots of the people in the neighborhood where we sat that morning would have thought about going to church on

Sunday morning, but that inclination is pretty much gone. Not so long ago I had pastored a church filled with people. But on this Sunday I was sitting with my coffee at a garage sale, holding my little grandson and watching the steady stream of shoppers. I and a host of others of all ages had chosen to go to a garage sale rather than church.

As I watched the congregating people, they seemed relaxed and happy. They were enjoying each other and seemed to be having the kind of "family" experience that's supposed to happen in the enlarged foyers of those big, new, seeker-sensitive churches. I wondered about these people and myself. How had we gotten here? What changes had occurred that made us all comfortable with this way of spending Sunday morning? The way of life we have known for so long is being reordered by the deep, disturbing changes that continue to gather force. What is church in this context? What is the gospel in this place, at this time, among these people? These were the questions I considered that Sunday morning, while at the same time a part of me wanted to kneel before the table and be fed by the One who said: "This is my body."

Like a whole lot of other people, I feel as though I'm in the midst of a great rolling sea that is sinking and rising all around me. Profound changes are afoot, gathering force, disrupting our habits and comfortable way of life. Climate change is one thing, but the accelerating loss of the Christian narrative across the emerging generations is quite another. Movements of peoples across the globe and global economic forces cause most of us to feel like pawns with no ability to control what happens to us.

These disruptions are huge and disturbing, and their impact will be to make us very different kinds of human beings. I confess little idea about what this might mean, but I can sense greater changes coming that will have a major impact not only on individuals but on the church. What is God up to in the midst of all this? It is essential for us to understand so that we can bring change to the church in this world where everything is changing.

Asking Different Questions

The questions we're asking and the experiences we're undergoing aren't new. Christians across millennia have had to ask hard questions about the nature of Christian life in their times. I remember sitting at a coffee shop one Monday morning after a very "successful" Sunday when the worship worked, the church was full, and people were excited about their experience in song, drama, video presentation, and the sermon.

While sitting in the coffee shop, I overheard a conversation between a man and woman about a retreat he had just been to on one of the San Juan Islands off the coast of Vancouver. They were talking about finding spiritual moorings in a world that was ever more complicated and unmanageable, a concern that never seems to be on the radar of the people crowding into the church on Sunday morning, who often come just to experience contemporary music and a service that makes them feel good. I knew that the raw stories I was overhearing could be describing a lot of people who had been in my church the day before. The struggles my congregation faced were no different from the concerns of those two people, yet the people in my church never talked about their struggles.

I started asking: *How might we create the kinds of safe spaces where the real stories shaping people's lives become the ones we own and address in our churches? How do we do church better on Sunday so that it is more relevant to where these people are? How do we get these people in the coffee shop to church on Sunday?* Then I realized my questions were all wrong. They were my default questions, church questions. I hardly ever stopped long enough to listen to the people, because when they voiced their concerns, I was busy trying to come up with strategies to get them to come to my church. Too often church questions reveal the "seeker church" mentality and result in a search for successful techniques to draw people to the church as if the church is the answer to every question.

I remember being near a national pastors conference a few years ago, which is to say I was speaking at a different conference meeting in the same building. As I was walking toward an elevator, a Mennonite pastor was walking toward me—his conference nametag gave away his identity. As we got on the elevator together, I asked him, "What's a Mennonite pastor doing at a conference like this?" He asked me what I meant. I responded, "Well, these conferences are all about pragmatic programs and solutions to make the church work and get people into the pews. You come from a tradition with a very different understanding of church." He looked at me and said, "That's why I'm here. Because it works." My heart sank.

From the beginnings of the church, Christians have needed to figure out how to ask different kinds of questions about what the Spirit is up to among them. Over and over again within the pages of the New Testament, we see what seemed like a settled issue of the gospel's place in a particular time and among a particular culture suddenly become something that could no longer be taken for granted. Questions that seemed settled had to be asked all over again. Luke-Acts is a case in point. In Acts the Spirit continually upended the settled assumptions of Jewish and Gentile Christians in terms of what it meant to be God's people in their time and place. In the midst of huge challenges, we too are confronted with questions about what it means to be God's people.

At that garage sale, sitting with little Owen in my arms, sipping my coffee, and watching the people around me, I knew our time for addressing these questions had come. I knew the answers were not new methods for getting people to come to church or even plans for reaching seekers. These answers lead us down all the wrong paths and miss the point of the gospel. When we are truly seeking to know what it means to be God's people, we will want to know what God is up to in our neighborhoods and communities and what it means for the gospel to be lived out and proclaimed in this time and place. The matter of getting someone to church is utterly secondary to these insights. Now we are in a place where ecclesiology isn't the issue. Missiology is.

Heirs to the Reformation

A problem we face is that since the sixteenth century our questions have been shaped by the Reformation. While a momentous upheaval in the Western church and a turning point in the self-understanding of human life at the dawn of the modern era, the Reformation resulted in a focus that still controls our imagination—a focus on church questions that are no longer helpful in the missionary situation that confronts us.

Irrespective of the theological creativity that might have framed the Reformers, both Magisterial and Radical, as they thought about the nature of grace, the role of Scripture, or the human capacities to respond to God in faith, they assumed that the church should be at the center of culture and that the right forms of teaching, liturgy, and the ordering of ministry were of primary importance.

This is not a criticism of how late-Medieval and protomodern forms of religious life in Europe were institutionalized. Protestant life emerging in Europe post-Westphalia, and later in North American denominationalism exported around the world, was about the proper forms of church, the right forms of clergy, and the right understanding of the gospel for a specific church group. Perhaps without intention but certainly in practice, Protestant life was largely about getting these things right.

This is illustrated in the ways in which the basic tenets of Protestant life were put into place after the Reformation. Take, for example, basic notions of clergy. Overall, the fundamental change that occurred was in the nature of the clerical role, and the Protestant resolution was to turn a fundamentally sacerdotal, priestly role into a teaching role—removing priestly vestments and replacing them with teacher's robes.

This was consistent with the new definition of the church as a *place* where the *right* teaching of the Word took place and the *right* administration of the sacraments occurred and the *right* forms of discipline were carried out. Over the centuries some of these basic images may have shifted and changed (such as more focus on the pastoral-therapeutic role or the manager-entrepreneurial role), but the basic orientation has been toward getting the church "right" and ensuring that the right forms and functions of church be carried out by the right (credentialed) people in the right places.

The sixteenth-century Reformation bequeathed us a set of questions concerning the Christian life that were largely church questions, and they still shape our imagination. Whether in a traditional denomination or one of the newer, supposedly more culturally sensitive groups—such as seeker or simple or emergent—the same basic question directs conversation and practice, namely, What kind of church do we need and how do we make that kind of church work? By centering on such questions we remain captive to an imagination that is the direct heir of a pre- and post-Eurocentric Reformation culture.

Looking to Luke

Where can we turn to find a different way of addressing the challenges of this unthinkable world where the expected and assumed narratives about how things ought to work have failed? Where are the examples of how Christians have wrestled with this situation and responded to it in radically different ways from that of the Reformation heritage? The New Testament is, in fact, an example of diverse groups of Christians addressing unthinkable worlds but learning to ask profoundly different kinds of questions. One of the most helpful theologians, interpreters, and historiographers of the early church is Luke. He demonstrates how to ask questions that are more fundamental than the European–North American, post-Reformation, ecclesiocentric questions we've been asking. Most important, he is addressing how to discern what God is up to in this world.

Of the four Gospel writers, only Luke was not a Jew. He's writing to people living outside the geography of Palestine after the period in which the events of the Gospels and Acts are narrated, probably toward the end of the first century. By the time he writes, immense shifts have already taken place in the life of the young Christian movement. Assumptions about its focus and direction have been shattered. The Jewish/Jerusalem-centered community, shaped so profoundly by its long narrative history of God's dealings with them, has been displaced. Luke's audience is people who have learned secondhand the events recorded in the Gospels and Acts—eyewitnesses are gone. They are Gentile Christian communities living in a world in which mystical spiritualities flooding in from India and Egypt are competing with the Greek and Roman gods, who seemed to have lost their power to hold people's loyalties.

For some, in the swirl of these tides, Jesus and the God of the Jewish people seemed small, alien, and irrelevant. Luke's two little volumes, Luke and Acts, are addressed to young Christians who aren't concerned about worship style or musical type. These are confused people questioning what God is up to in their world. They wonder why so many of the promises of this new gospel have failed to materialize, such as Jesus's return to Jerusalem and the Roman Empire bowing its knee to the Lord. They found themselves in an unthinkable time. What had happened to the Christian story? What were they to do about it?

Who were the people Luke addressed? He writes to one named Theophilus—a man who knew about the events of Jesus's life, death, and resurrection, and who also knew that Jerusalem had been destroyed and its citizens scattered over the earth. By the time Luke wrote his two volumes, the Jewish people had clearly rejected the claims of the Jesus sect, branding it as incompatible with their tradition and faith.

Luke told Theophilus that his volumes would be an "orderly account" of the events of Jesus's life and what had resulted from the movement that his death and resurrection birthed (Luke 1:1–2 NRSV). Luke is intending to set out a history meant to assure Theophilus that these events are true and therefore a story on which a person can base his life. Theophilus must have been a Greek-speaking believer who, like many of his background, was struggling to make sense of the massive shifts that had so quickly and completely overtaken and transformed the early Christian communities and their expectations.

As we read Luke's writings, let's listen attentively in ways that will seem quite strange and counterintuitive to much of how we ordinarily read him. Luke addressed people shaken out of settled assumptions about the Jesus movement and what God is up to in the world. These were men and women, much like many of us reading this book, who had been cast into a tumultuous, pluralistic world that turned settled assumptions upside down. Luke does not write a generic book but one that addresses specific, small communities of Christians who were struggling to make sense of their faith.

In this book I will focus on several sections of Luke's Gospel (particular attention is given to Luke 10:1–12) and some of the early events in the book of Acts. In these texts there are clues to how we might respond to our questions.

2

A Parable of Three Friends

Coming to a Right Understanding of Newbigin

Once there were three friends who grew up together. From child-hood their lives were intertwined in play, at school, on the street, and in their dreaming. Their relationship made them inseparable. They had different personalities and even their approaches to life were quite divergent, but they were bound together like the Hobbits in *Lord of the Rings*.

At college they shared a rich intellectual and social life and on many a long evening they would talk at length, sharing their hearts, listening to each other's dreams, and making plans to change the world. Amid laughter, hard work, confusion, and sometimes pain, they experienced moments of exhilaration when friend listened to friend or celebrated what the other had accomplished. Through all those years they learned to connect in ways that hardly required words. Their relationship was their strength; it shaped their identi-ties. Sometimes they were very close, at other times distant, sometimes argumentative, other times partners in projects. But they were bound as one.

As with many relationships of youth, when they grew older, they gradually moved apart. Following college, each married and found jobs in different cities; their times together became more sporadic and episodic. They would still connect by phone and internet; it was easy for them to become Facebook friends, but the long conversations became rare events.

Every few years they'd meet for a weekend, and then it was as if they'd never been apart. Once again they shared the dreams and longings of their hearts. In the brief hours of a weekend, they heard and understood each other as no one else could.

But time has a way of changing so much. Life, through its rhythms and patterns, shapes us in ways few of us ever expect or plan. Somehow we lose touch with those who've been so important to us. It's never intentional but it happens. And this is what the three friends experienced. They grew away from the relationships that had once been such a vital part of their lives.

Then one day, quite unexpectedly, two of the friends received emails from the third. The email came as a wonderful surprise. The third friend invited them to spend a weekend at his home on the West Coast, offering a few long evenings of food, wine, and conversations like the ones they remembered. It sounded perfect.

The two made plans to travel west. They looked forward to being able to tell each other the ongoing stories of their lives, picking up from where they all left off years before.

When they arrived at their friend's home, their host welcomed them eagerly. The evening began with catching up about families and jobs. They joked about weight and age and they talked about old times. The food was great and obviously the host had learned a lot about the vintages and pairing of wine.

But sometime during the evening the atmosphere changed. It was hard to pinpoint the moment, but the two invited friends began to sense something was wrong. They couldn't put their finger on what it was at first, but each sensed an unease and disquiet entering the conversation. An unspoken awkwardness set in as if two sets of in-laws-to-be were meeting each other for the first time and the conversation became strained.

The host began doing the talking and it was all about himself. Each time the friends spoke, the host cut them off and turned the conversation back to his life, his questions, and his needs. He asked lots of questions to elicit information that would further focus on his own interests and plans. He mined them for information that could make him look better. He seemed preoccupied with how to become more successful.

For him the evening was a wonderful, enjoyable, successful time. He felt great! The other two felt like objects being used to meet someone else's needs.

As soon as they could, the two invited guests said they needed to get back to their hotel. They thanked their old friend and departed, perplexed and sad. What had happened? How could their friend have become so self-absorbed?

Each time I share this parable with church leaders, I get strange looks and lots of silence. "Who are these three friends, and what do they have to do with the question of what it means for the gospel to be lived out and proclaimed in this time and place?" they ask.

Several years ago in Australia I began a lecture series with this parable and could tell immediately I'd created a lot of anxiety in the room. Few of the two hundred pastors assembled there seemed to understand what I was getting at. I confess my sadness at the response. I needed someone to let me know they understood, that I wasn't alone with the questions that keep shaping my imagination. But that day it wasn't to be.

Following the telling of this parable I said to the pastors gathered at the conference that I would not be speaking about the church and would not answer any questions about church. As they headed for their tea break, a disquieting murmur filled the hall. In fact, as the lectures went on, I became more and more aware of how few leaders actually understand the nature of the crisis we face. Few leaders recognize, despite all their conversations about a post-Christian and missional church, that they are deeply embedded in some of the most powerful imaginations of modernity.

The Journey of Lesslie Newbigin

What is the parable about? To answer that question I need to share something of how my thinking has been shaped over the past decade. Ten years ago I participated in writing the book *Missional Church*.[1] The book's imagination was shaped by the work of Lesslie Newbigin. This parable is a response to a conviction in me that, when the book was written, I failed to hear fully what Newbigin was saying. Subsequently, as I have watched, listened, and read the ways people have engaged the missional conversation, I have realized the depth of my captivity to the functional Christendom that *Missional Church* critiqued.

By now Lesslie Newbigin's story is a familiar one. Even so, to explain the parable, it's important to trace some of the contours of that story. For more than thirty years, Newbigin was a missionary in India, where he served as a founding bishop in the Church of South India.[2]

He left for India as a missionary in the late thirties when the English church was still focused on the question of how to put back together a kind of Christendom world. Following the end of World War I, Christians harbored anxiety about the loss of the Christian narrative from the center of culture. Conferences were assembled, papers given, and books written on how to remake Christian England. In the midst of this hand-wringing and ferment, Newbigin was completing his university training and preparing for life as a missionary.

From the beginning of his time in India, Newbigin knew he was an outsider who needed to listen to and learn the cultures of that vast country's peoples. He would do this by sitting in villages with local religious leaders and they would read each other's sacred texts. Then Newbigin made a discovery: he needed to relearn the gospel itself. He realized he hadn't come to India just to convert the Indian people. As he lived among these people, he realized that the gospel was converting him; it was questioning some of his most basic assumptions.

This need to relearn, or rediscover, the gospel was not about some liberal-conservative conflict, nor was it a crisis of faith. Because he was constantly compelled to read the gospel from the perspective of the other, he was being taken ever more deeply into its implications. Newbigin was always a deeply evangelical, orthodox Christian, but in India he came to understand the extent of his captivity to the canons of modernity and the West and his assumption that these canons were the right and only ways of reading the gospel. He discovered he could not simply arrive in India, learn the language, and then "give" the gospel as if it were some disembodied, abstract set of propositions that, like a Lego piece, can be plugged in anywhere. India required him to hear and read the gospel all over again in ways he would not have discovered had he stayed in the United Kingdom. Sitting with learned Indian spiritual leaders, as well as ordinary village people, Newbigin was driven ever more deeply into the study of the Scriptures to relearn what was there. In this sense, he was dwelling in the Word as he dwelt among a people.

In the seventies he returned to an England radically altered from the one he had left so many years earlier. In the twenties and thirties at Oxford, he had been shaped in and by a Christian England where all about him people lived inside the assumptions and habits of a Christian tradition. In the seventies he encountered an England that had left that narrative behind, except in some of its external trappings and traditions. For all practical purposes the life of ordinary

English people was no longer even vaguely Christian. His country was now a pervasively pluralistic society, with a variety of religious and ethnic groups. The shock of this sea change after almost thirty years away caused Newbigin to ask disturbing questions about the nature of the gospel because the country that had once sent him out as a missionary had itself become a mission field.

Newbigin had already experienced this changed reality in very personal ways. Paul Weston, in a biographical introduction to his Newbigin reader, describes the two-month land journey the Newbigins took on their return home from India. They traveled through Pakistan, Russia, and Turkey, then over into Cappadocia, once a center of Christian intellectual and cultural life. Weston describes their experience:

> [It] turned out to be the only place on the entire trip where the New-bigins had to worship on their own on Sunday because they could find no other Christians with whom to share fellowship. This had a profound effect upon Lesslie and helped to energize his reflections on European culture, for it brought home just how completely a once-strong Christian heritage could all but disappear.[3]

Newbigin describes some of this shock in one of the first pieces he wrote after returning to the United Kingdom. *The Other Side of 1984* begins with a description of Western youth in India:

> Before we left India in 1974 we had become accustomed to the sight of young people from affluent homes in England, France and Germany roaming the streets in tattered and unwashed Indian clothes, having turned their backs on Europe in the hope that—even as beggars—they might find in India something to make life worth living. . . . In subsequent years of ministry in England I have often been asked: "What is the greatest difficulty you faced in moving from India to England?" I have always answered: "The disappearance of hope."

He then summarizes these observations with this statement: "It is, no doubt, easy in every age to point to its obvious weaknesses. What is in question here, however, is something more precise. It is the dramatic suddenness with which, in the space of one lifetime, our civilization has so completely lost confidence in is own validity."[4]

During his career, Newbigin worked as a missiologist with World Council of Churches. He was well acquainted with the dominant theological figures of the twentieth century (Karl Barth was an attender at numerous meetings and theological conferences held by the WCC), as well as the massive transformations in the Western understanding of the missiological task. Confronted with a United Kingdom so radically different from the one he'd left, the shock raised for him a startling but fundamental question: *Can the West be converted?* This question shaped the rest of his life until he died in the late nineties.

Part of Newbigin's legacy is that his best, most creative work occurred after he was sixty-five. Retirement was the beginning of a new vocation as he sought to understand and engage his own country from the perspective of a cross-cultural missionary. His whole life to that point, it seemed, was preparation for those last twenty-plus years. He wrote his best and most lucid work in those years. Even after going blind, he spoke with such a prophetic lucidity, people knew they were hearing words that spoke to the core of our time. Someone would sit with him each day reading complicated works of philosophy and social theory; then he would dictate the pages of the book *The Gospel in a Pluralist Society*. It was the mature work of an aged man that gave many Christians intellectual and theological bearings with which to understand the challenge of Christian witness in our time.[5]

Professor Colin Green, who knew Newbigin during that period, tells of attending a meeting at which Newbigin spoke, only four or so months before his death. Without notes he described accurately the situation of Christian life in the West. Green describes how leaders of the church in the United Kingdom sat silent, riveted, with tears in their eyes, knowing they were listening for the last time to a man of God who saw the reality of the times and framed it in a powerful and compelling manner. He was a prophet in our time.

Across the generations Newbigin was loved and heeded. In old age he was a luminous guidepost for many. In the eighties I attended a Lausanne Theological Study group in Uppsala, Sweden, on the question of postmodernism, the gospel, and culture. Newbigin was one of the presenters. By then he was known around the world. He was slowing down and didn't want to be away from his wife for too long, but he was engaged in all that was going on at the conference.

One evening he asked to come to supper with a group of us. At that supper table, we saw the grace of one who receives, welcomes, and blesses the other. Newbigin spent the evening asking us questions and listening intently to what we had to say, wanting to learn from a younger generation. I was struck by his grace and desire to learn.

I'll remember that evening for the rest of my life, how such a gracious and just saint sat with me, asked questions, and listened to me. I have much to learn from his spirit and I thank God for those few hours with him in conversation. It was a meal I wasn't ready to leave.

Newbigin's Agenda

In his writing from the mid-sixties forward, Newbigin asked a question about Western culture from the perspective of a missiologist. It can be stated as follows: *What is a missional encounter with this culture?* He too needed to struggle with the question of Christian life in the strange new world where the Christian story no longer shaped people's lives. As a cross-cultural missionary to India, he was able to see the Christian crisis in the West as an insider with the eyes of an outsider. He argued that the gospel would reengage the West if the church and its leaders became "cross-cultural" missionaries in their own cultures. He sought to answer this question: How does the gospel engage a culture that is radically different from one's own when that culture is now one's own?

In this light I want to address three of Newbigin's books, because they illustrate the point I want to make, the meaning behind my parable. The books are *The Open Secret*, *Foolishness to the Greeks*, and *The Gospel in a Pluralist Society*. I will discuss them in the order of their publication because they represent some thirty years of dialogue Newbigin had as a missionary in the country that once sent him to India.

In these books we encounter a critical theme I missed until a few years ago in my reading of him. I think I understand the reason I missed it for so long, as I read these books at one level, not getting what he was saying to Christians in the West. I will hold off discussing that reason until after summarizing some themes in each book.

The Open Secret

The Open Secret[6] was written early on when Newbigin taught at Selly Oaks in Birmingham. It was a training manual in biblical theology for missionaries preparing to go overseas. Put into its current form in the seventies, it is simple in outline but profound in its argument that a missional imagination is at the heart of the God of the Bible. The primary theme is the work of God in the world, and underlying it all is the paramount notion of *election* as the key to understanding the nature of the kingdom of God and its mission in the world. For Newbigin, election meant that we as Christians have been called to a vocation in Christ for the sake of God's world.

Foolishness to the Greeks

Foolishness to the Greeks[7] was based on Newbigin's 1984 Princeton Lectures on the challenge of mission in the modern narrative. It is a tract—a response to the "shock" of reentering a culture no longer one's own. Here the mature missiologist is firing well-aimed arguments across the bows of modernity. The prose is deceptively simple, but the argument is sustained and perceptive. Behind this book is the mind of a practical missiologist shaped by the intellectual currents of the twentieth century. In it a bishop of the church—a faithful, practicing theologian—enters deeply into the intellectual milieu of his time. Too many leaders today have a hard time understanding this book. They struggle to follow its argument and grasp its basic ideas. Most have never been given the basic foundations for understanding the intellectual and cultural history of the modern West that represents a huge challenge to forming communities of the kingdom in our context.

I'm writing this in a little mountain village in Tuscany called Roccatederighi, twenty miles from Siena, one of the main cities of the Renaissance. Siena, with its ringed walls around the great piazza and the two duomos, is a treasure of history. Earlier I was standing in the baptistry of one of the duomos with its amazing ceiling frescos used to teach people the Apostles' Creed. On the walls were paintings that taught the gospel stories. In the center of the room is a beautiful baptismal font created in the fifteenth century. The drama of salvation is inscribed in Latin around the font. These images and symbols were once a normal part of a young person's education in the West. When Newbigin went to school in the early part of the last century, it was simply the air one breathed. When he left Oxford, he was steeped in the Western tradition. Newbigin's shock was, in part, that, when he returned to his homeland, this tradition had, in so short a time, all but disappeared from people's imagination.

On a hot mid-August afternoon, the duomo baptistery was filled with tourists from Europe and North America. I was aware of how few had any sense of what was in the room—their history, tradition, and past. Listening to conversations, it was clear to me that these were simply tourists seeing all they could see, snapping a few more photos before moving on to the next attraction.

Newbigin must have had a similar experience when he returned to the United Kingdom from India. He recognized that the Christian story had all but been lost to most English citizens, and he knew what an immense loss this was. *Foolishness to the Greeks* is a Tractarian accounting of the forces and beliefs shaping recent Western imagination and a critique of its failure. In this book he wrestled with his culture as one who needed to understand what caused it so quickly to remove the Christian story from its center.

The Gospel in a Pluralist Society

The Gospel in a Pluralist Society was published in 1989. It moves beyond a Tractarian moment into a critical conversation with basic sources of the Western tradition. Newbigin names key challenges the gospel must now engage in the West, going into detail about the new culture of pluralism. It is a wonderfully sustained argument and a deeply reflective book, important because of what Newbigin is up to in its pages. Again it reflects a missionary working hard to understand his cultural context with all its tradition and history so that he can engage that culture in a dialogue concerning Scripture and the Christian story.

If we are to get a handle on the challenges of the multiple pluralisms facing us today, we will need to listen to people in places like the garage sale with the passion and energy Newbigin used in his own context. I imagine that, as he wrote *The Gospel in a Pluralist Society*, he spent time walking through the streets of his familiar Birmingham, listening to the sounds of change.

Little more than a century earlier, just around the corner from where Newbigin had taught at Selly Oaks and now lived in his retirement, was the original Cadbury chocolate factory founded in the nineteenth century by the Cadbury family, who were devout Christians. Cadbury, out of his Christian convictions, built the model town of Bournville where most of his workers and their families lived. It was a community of small cottagelike homes surrounded by parks and green space with a town square occupied by library and church.

It was a model imagination for a Christian world of work, home, and worship. Just a five-minute walk from where Newbigin lived, it must have been in his thoughts as he observed his own community, a radically changed world with its multiplicity of nations, peoples, and religions. We're all in a similar world.

What I Missed

I want to return to the parable in relationship to what I missed for too long in these books because I was preoccupied with the wrong issues and asking the wrong questions. First, I'll state it positively, then negatively, to get at the parable's meaning.

Positively

As a missiologist, Newbigin's consistent focus in his writing over thirty years involved a continual wrestling with the question of how the gospel engages the culture of the modern West. He was in a constant dialogue with the culture, in which he lived, and the gospel, which he loved. It was a back-and-forth dialogue, not one-way. Reading these books is to know one is listening in on someone who has spent time immersed in, listening to, and loving this culture in which he is embedded. It's striking how Newbigin doesn't use this culture to get somewhere else—he indwells it and through that indwelling reads again the biblical narratives to ask how the gospel could reengage his culture in his time.

I don't think most Christian leaders in North America do anything like that. This is why Newbigin was such a gift—he practiced a different conversation than do most of us who are in the church.

Negatively

The church is not the focus of Newbigin's attention and questions. Questions about being the church are, in Newbigin's books, secondary to and follow from the question of a missional engagement of Scripture with the cultural context in which we are located. Again, it sounds so simple as to be obvious and not requiring comment. But this observation is crucial to what I want to say.

In making this point I'm not suggesting the church was unimportant for Newbigin, but it was not the primary category that engaged his imagination. Let me illustrate. *The Gospel in a Pluralist Society* contains the oft-quoted chapter "The Church as the Hermeneutic of the Gospel." When I discuss this book, church leaders immediately quote the chapter title, believing this is the primary illustration of what Newbigin is doing in the book.

This chapter is part of the book's conclusion, coming at the end of a series of questions about the relationship between Scripture, the gospel, and this culture of late modernity. Because the church is not the focus of the book, the discussion about the church comes at the end. This was the point I missed for so long. I kept coming to Newbigin's books with "church" questions looking for "church" answers, and by so doing, I missed the genius and energy of his work.

Scripture, Church, and Culture

Newbigin understood and modeled the engagement between Scripture, gospel, and culture in ways most church leaders still have difficulty recognizing. The attention of too many leading writers and thinkers is still focused in one of two directions. On the one side are attempts to fix the church under the rubric of renewal or transformation. There appears to be an overwhelming conviction that if we, first, get the idea of the church right in terms of descriptions, organizational systems, and definitions, the rest will fall into place. The problem is that we won't address questions about the nature and function of the church by starting with questions about the church. In the changed contexts of our time, starting with church questions (whether multisite churches, the renaissance of the church, the whole church, church morph, sticky church, or church turned inside out or whatever) takes us in all the wrong directions because they are the same old kinds of questions we've been asking since before the Reformation.[8]

On the other side are those who want to set aside the church as it exists (of course there is no other kind of church) as being irrelevant or past bothering with. This is never expressed directly, but some of those who use the missional conversation and seek to articulate ways of following Jesus are part of this antichurch stance.

Each of these is mentioned to make it clear that the argument of this book is not antichurch. In fact, my argument is born out of a passionate desire for local churches to embrace the *missio Dei* in their neighborhoods and communities.

The heart of this book is to address these questions: What is God up to in our neighborhoods and communities? What is the nature of an engagement between the biblical imagination and this place where we find ourselves, at this time, among these people? What then will a local church look like when it responds to such questions?

Notice the focus and direction of these questions. They are not primarily about the church, its inner functions and processes, or its ideal identity and nature. They are about God and how God relates to our neighborhoods. Focusing on church questions, on what it means to be the church, is akin to the search for happiness. Just as one will not get far on the road to happiness by predefining the characteristics of happiness and then going to look for them, we will not grasp what it means to be the church in our time by beginning with church questions, even if they are questions about the church's health, effectiveness, or its natural development!

Newbigin moved in a different direction. This book proposes that part of the reason Newbigin has never really been understood or his insights accepted by the church in North America is because people have assumed that his focus was on issues of ecclesiology and the question of how to make the church more effective in a late modern culture. This is a profound misinterpretation. As I have said, in the formation of a missional movement of the people of God, questions about the church cannot be the starting point, but this is the propensity of Christian leaders. This preoccupation suggests the continuing depths of our colonization to a Christendom imagination. Christendom was, in part, about the church at the center of the conversation. We haven't realized the extent to which we continue to live there.

I read book after book sent to me by publishers for examination. Too often what shapes them are these questions of how to make the church work, how to move churches from inside to outside, how to . . . This is our norm. It's how most pastors and ministers are trained to think, and it represents a problematic captivity that must be addressed if we, like Newbigin, are to wrestle with the nature of the gospel in and for and with and, at times, against, our culture. In the interplay between Scripture, church, and culture, our predisposition is to think first and foremost in terms of church questions—Scripture and culture have become secondary to and a function of the church effectiveness questions. Like a frustrating computer program, we keep returning to the preset position, assuming it's the correct place to be.

Martin Robinson, the director of Together in Mission in the United Kingdom, has reflected on this situation from the United Kingdom–European perspective in a series of conversations we have had together with Dr. Colin Greene. Martin and Colin cowrote the book *Metavista*,[9] which is a wonderful framing of the challenges to mission being faced in that context. Martin described something of the trajectory that has been followed by the Protestant churches in the United Kingdom and Europe. The following is a simplified outline generalizing his assessment of what has taken place since the beginning of the twentieth century.

1914–1945	**Repairing Christianity** The shock of WWI and the intervening years brought about numbers of major conferences (for example, Oxford in 1937) and books seeking to engage the crisis of Christianity by repairing what seemed broken to put the church back on track. This was perceived as a need to repair and return, not make fundamental adaptations.
1950s–1960s	**"We Have Succeeded"** The postwar euphoria briefly created a moment during which the church was put back on track. But this was only the calm at the eye of the hurricane; it was a brief time before the full fury of culture change hit.
1970s–2000s	**Can We Survive?** Loss of faith in the Christian narrative post-WWII alongside the rising tides of nominalism and secularity resulted in a massive loss of confidence in and commitment to the church. The question was answered, finally, by a whispered, "Yes, but only as a minority." This was the church to which Newbigin returned. His attention, however, was not on the church as much as it was on the cultural forces that had created this situation.
2000s	**We Have to Reengage Our Culture(s)** A growing recognition that without a willingness to move our focus from church questions to radical listening in engagement with the culture and to biblical imagination, there will be no missional life. This is more than a tactical shift of focus; it is a fundamental change in social imagination. In the United Kingdom and Europe, the issue is now about the reconstitution of culture, not the fixing of the church.

It should be noted from this simple overview that right up until very recently the focus of conversation remained on the church question. Only as Christians began to grasp that the issue was no longer about fixing the church but about the reengagement with a culture that had birthed the Christian narrative in the West could there be missional engagement. The story in North America is quite different from that in the United Kingdom and Europe, but the issue is the same. One can create a different but parallel summary of the North American church over the same period of time.

1914–1945	**Church as Consolidation and Expansion of Denominationalism** In North America the church grew and thrived. The focus was on organizational rationalization to be better equipped to continue the growth coming from immigration. The denominations are largely a Euro-tribal culture reflecting the demographics of the continent. It was a clericalist church, with growing emphasis on the proper credentials in terms of education and identity.
1950s–1970s	**Church as Corporate Denomination** Denominationalism is at its height. The church has succeeded in engaging the suburbanization of culture and the postwar generation with cradle-to-grave programs through a corporatist, franchise-based organization run by managers and professionals.
1970s–2000s	**Church as Rationalized Technical Success** This is an era of religious winners and losers as mainline churches fail to grasp the cultural shifts of the sixties and evangelicals and charismatics win the culture wars in terms of growth. The primary approach to an emerging cultural upheaval are technical, rational approaches to adjust, renew, and fix the church through such movements as church growth, church effectiveness, and church health.
1990s–2000s	**Awakening to the Shifts in Culture** There is a gradual recognition that the culture has shifted. Attempts are made to address this with new methods of being the church, such as the emergent movement and the missional church. This shift, however, is mostly a change in form rather than substance. The focus remains on how to fix the church in a changing culture. Church questions continue to shape the environment.

The Parable Explained

This brings us, finally, back to the parable. The three friends are Scripture, culture, and church. For some fifteen hundred years they grew together, becoming deeply intertwined in the Western imagination. At times one was more dominant than the others, but they remained connected to one another. They've been sundered—so far apart have they grown that they hardly recognize each other anymore. Each has shaped its own life, now often over against the other. And when the three come together, there is a profound disconnect, because one of the three has lost any sense of perspective or understanding of importance and place. In its effort to avoid being left out and its need to look relevant, one sees itself as the most important conversation partner.

The only questions the church asks of the culture are church questions: How do I get information and data about this culture to make the church successful? And when the church comes to the biblical narratives, it is there only to ask church questions: What are the biblical criteria for a successful church? What does the Bible say about the church and its purpose? What are the guidelines for church health? What are the principles, values, and techniques for making the marriages of our people successful? and so on. When we engage Scripture and our cultural contexts, it isn't a dialogue; the church is always holding up a mirror that reflects back its own image. This ecclesiocentric obsession means that primarily we mine both Scripture and culture for our own needs. We're so preoccupied with church questions that neither biblical narratives nor culture can become the places where God addresses us and challenges us to be converted.

Newbigin was never preoccupied with church questions. This is the reason his books are such a breath of fresh air—he indwelt both Scripture and the cultures in which he lived, not to use them as ends but out of a deeply incarnational engagement.

How will we indwell both the gospel and the people in neighborhoods where we live and work so that we hear God speak to us in and through them? Before moving too quickly to answers, I want to share a little more of the journey that has brought me to realize that church questions can only misdirect.

3

How It All Came to Be

A Brief History of the Missional Conversation

A Movement Is Born

In the late seventies and early eighties, a new movement was formed in North America around Newbigin's question: what is a missionary engagement with Western culture in our time? The Gospel and Our Culture Network (GOCN) was the creative, energetic child of a group of younger American seminary educators and church leaders aware that Newbigin's observations in England were becoming the reality of the North American church. While the contexts were not the same and the development of denominational life in North America was significantly different, it became clear to these leaders that this continent had also entered its own missionary situation. They recognized that Newbigin had named the conversation in terms of a dynamic, cross-cultural engagement between the church, gospel, and culture. The North American GOCN formed around this agenda but determined that it would initially focus its energy on the ecclesiological side of that three-way dialogue.

In the late seventies I had just completed eight years of pastoral ministry in a small town outside Toronto. By all the established measures it had been a success. I had gone to the congregation following their unpleasant experience with the former pastor and I saw the church grow back to health with lots of young families coming. We did some adventuresome things together, such as sponsoring fifty Southeast Asian refugees. We invited them into our homes and helped get them established in jobs and homes of their own.

Some members formed a nonprofit corporation, bought an apartment building, and gradually turned it over to a group of single moms and others struggling economically. We learned from Mary Cosby, of the Church of the Saviour in Washington, D.C., about the inward and outward journey. At the same time there were forces wanting to return the church to what they considered a more "normal" and "traditional" way, which meant filling pews with people who thought and acted pretty much the way they did.

I was aware of a new dynamic all about me in this small town. It was growing rapidly with young couples who couldn't afford the high prices of housing in Toronto. The old town was becoming an exurbia for these younger families. As this happened, the experience of an old market town (Newmarket was the name of the town) was disappearing.

I was aware that by the late seventies in Canada it was still easy to grow a church, but the growth came from people moving from other churches that didn't meet their needs. I struggled with this recognition, knowing that my generation had pretty much written off the church as an irrelevant institution with nothing to say to an emerging culture.

Canada experienced this shift in the seventies. It was, for me, a period of searching for direction and conversation partners who knew that the most boring thing in the world was to grow churches filled with Christians coming from other churches. I looked for conversation partners who could help me come to terms with the fact that those of my generation were no longer interested in or had any real memory of the Christian story. How could I get a handle on this reality that, if taken seriously, meant all the questions we were asking as churches had to be changed?

I found few conversation partners in my denomination. Returning to graduate school, I studied for three years with Jesuits, working hard at understanding the intellectual roots of the crisis I saw developing between the church and my culture. The Jesuits gave me the gift of intellectual frameworks rooted deeply in the traditions of the church. I also connected with people like Craig Van Gelder and George Hunsberger, who were forming the fledgling GOCN. Getting to know Craig and George was a great gift that came at an important point in my life; their insights and the community of the new network felt like coming home. I found conversation partners on this journey of understanding what it meant to be a cross-cultural missionary in one's own culture. I owe a huge debt to people like George and Craig as well as Wilbert Shenk, who was leading a transatlantic study group on Newbigin's work. This was a period of rich dialogue and learning with a company of men and women who lent their imagination to the emerging conviction that we are in a new time and must learn again how to be on mission in our own culture.

Early on, GOCN developed a helpful framework for the conversation about a missional life within the changing context of religious life on this continent. It called for a *trialogue* (a three-way conversation) between gospel, church, and culture.

Its intent was to communicate that the way forward involved the cultivation of a series of dialogues that moved back and forth among the three points of the triangle. A helpful element of the diagram is that it doesn't give precedence to any one of the three over the others. It demonstrates that we cannot comprehend the gospel without engaging in an honest conversation with Bible and culture. Through the interaction of the three elements, we believed it was possible to hear the ways God was calling us to a missional engagement with our time and context.

Implicit in this model is a real and humble recognition that we cannot claim some a priori, privileged position in which we already "know" what the gospel is as we enter into dialogue with the culture and the church. While confessing that the Spirit bears witness to us in the midst of where we live and the culture(s) within which we are shaped, we acknowledge that the faithfulness of God through the Spirit has to work continually in, for, with, and against our specific cultural contexts. Through this model we were seeking to have a genuine three-way conversation.

In retrospect I don't think I (let me speak for myself, not the others to whom I may not have adequately listened) was at a place where I could have such a conversation. I didn't have the tools or resources to know how to go about it. But, more significantly, I remained locked into one side of the trialogue—it was the church questions that focused my attention. Because of this blinder, I simply was not capable of a genuine trialogue. I was the friend inviting the others to dinner to use them for my own ends.

GOCN created a conversation about a missionary engagement with North American culture through a series of publications. First, there was *The Church between Gospel and Culture*. Its title and structure were built around this three-way conversation. Next came *Missional Church: A Vision for the Sending of the Church in North America*, written by a team, including myself, over a three-year period. In this book we believed we were beginning to shape an ecclesiological conversation and offer important hints about a way forward. Then came a book comprised of a series of papers and articles called *Confident Witness—Changing World*, based on a conference we held in Chicago in 1997. The book and conference presented thought pieces around each of the three areas of gospel, culture, and church.

By this point, *Missional Church* was taking hold in the imagination of leaders in the United States, and the "missional church" language was becoming the lingua franca of conversation about the church. Other books emerged from various members of GOCN that demonstrated the rich, creative environment of the eighties and early nineties. I wrote *Liminality, Leadership and the Missional Church* as well as *Crossing the Bridge*. Both were books on the church and its leadership, picking up and developing themes found in *Missional Church*. Craig Van Gelder wrote *The Essence of the Church*, the first of a three-volume work on the nature and function of the church. Darrell Guder wrote *The Continuing Conversion of the Church* and another GOCN writing team published *Treasure in Clay Jars: Patterns of Missional Faithfulness*, focusing on congregations where elements of missional faithfulness at work could be seen.

Circling the Cul-de-sac

As I look back over those wonderfully invigorating years of dialogue, research, and experimenting in GOCN, I realize that, without any of us really reflecting on it, we ended up spending most of our time on church questions. Perhaps I am the only one who now sees it this way and I may have misread the emerging shape of the movement, but I think we ended up doing the very thing Newbigin did not do—we turned a trialogue into a monologue about the church. This monologue was about trying to understand the reasons the *church* had become captive to modernity; it was about the wrong turns the *church* had taken and the ways in which polity and structure had misguided the *church*; it was about alternative forms of leadership for the *church*; it was about how to understand the current malaise of the *church* in terms of systems and change. The focus of the conversation became the *church*. I believe this took us into a cul-de-sac as a movement, and now many use the *missional* language to describe anything they are doing in the *church*.

The focus has been on one side of the triangle at the expense of the other two. The ecclesial element, the conversation about missional *church*, has subsumed the other two within its agenda, so we see gospel and culture through the lens of *church*. This focus misses what is happening in the biblical narratives, and unless we turn away from this focus, we will not engage the people of our time and place—all the different cultures that now comprise our radically pluralistic society.

I don't want what I'm saying to be misconstrued. I'm not saying the church is unimportant. Quite the opposite! The church is vitally important to the mission of God. I'm saying we've not shed what others call a Christendom imagination where the church is basically the center of activity and conversation. Church questions are at the forefront of our thinking, so we default to questions about what the church should be doing and what the church should look like. This is a huge impediment to the development of a missionary people of God. This is not something that can be "fixed" with programs or discussions on church health or by appending the word *missional* to old habits.

Of Diets and New Directions

Most of us hear people talking often about the new diets they're trying for weight loss. My wife, Jane, bought a copy of O magazine (Oprah's monthly advice on how to get the right life for yourself) to read on the plane as we flew to London. She told me about a tongue-in-cheek article in which diets were determined according to one's Zodiac sign. There's no end to the mindless ways people look to cookbooks for ways to fix their bodies.

We all know that many people buy diet books, and most of the advice they offer is accurate and excellent. So the question that must be answered is, Why are so many people overweight if they're reading all these excellent diet books? The problem is that diet books can't do the one thing that's required: change the way we think about food and ourselves.

I connected with a dear friend in the United Kingdom over Skype after not seeing him for a while. I was struck by how much weight he had lost. He told me he'd lost several stone (a whimsical Briticism wonderfully based on human-sized measurement rather than the abstract metric system). What he said next caught my attention. He told me he started to lose weight only when he came to terms with the reality that he lived in and was part of a culture of consumerism in which to be is to consume. Only when he recognized this and chose to resist this narrative did he start seriously to lose weight.

Weight loss requires a deep change in our habits, attitudes, and actions over an extended period of time (one's whole life); it is about changing some fundamental beliefs about the focus of one's life. Without this, all the diet books in the world are a waste of time. Similarly, putting the word *missional* in front of all the church work we do will never get at the real challenge. We need new habits, attitudes, and actions around our relationship and engagements with the gospel and our cultures.

We have to stop talking about and asking church questions for quite a while. Only by doing this, as strange as it sounds, do we have a chance of discovering a church that can engage our time. Having said that, let me repeat again, as strongly as possible, the church is vitally important and at the heart of God's mission in the world. I am not church bashing. I love the church and am a part of a very concrete community of Christians in the Anglican Church. This is not about ganging up on the church but something radically different. The next chapter explores this perspective.

THE LANGUAGE HOUSE

A picture held us captive. . . . And we could not get outside of it, for it lay in our language and language seemed to repeat it to us inexorably.

Ludwig Wittgenstein, *Philosophical Investigations*

Language is the house of Being. In its home man dwells. Those who think and those who create with words are the guardians of this home.

Martin Heidegger, *Letter on Humanism*

The parable of the three friends described in part one is about the captivity of the church in the West to an imagination about its own place and role in the world. The word *imagination* expresses the fact that we do not go about articulating as a value the perspective presented in this parable. Indeed, a good many church leaders would be strongly averse to this articulation. The point here, however, is that beside, or beneath, our public declarations and theological confessions about the nature of the church, there lies a wholly different imagination about who we are and how we act in the world. As will be discussed in this part, some call this a "social imaginary" while others use the phrase "language house."

Stories That Shape Our Lives

Mark Lau Branson is a friend and associate who teaches at Fuller Seminary. We coteach a DMin cohort in missional leadership. Mark spent many years in Oakland, California, as part of a community of Christians who sought to make sense of being the church in their neighborhood. One of the things he had to address was how each person in this church and its surrounding community had been shaped.

> [We were] formed during late-modern consumerism . . . shaped by such priorities as individual choice, personal affectivity, and expectations (imaginations) that emphasized the pursuit of careers that should supply meaning and resources for our lives. We shared a growing conviction that these traits were being—or should be—questioned. In conversations, study, and prayer, we began a long journey of seeking alternatives.[1]

Mark's comments illustrate how we all live inside a particular story that tells how the world works and how we ought to live in it. In this case a group of Christians that began with the idea of shaping their church around their neighborhood quickly discovered that they were actually shaped by another story that cut through this ideal. This other story had to do with being individuals who, first, make their own personal, private choices and, second, determine how church might or might not impact these primary choices.

None of us decided at some point in our childhood or young adulthood that we would live inside a certain story of individualism or consumerism or careerism. We were born into a culture that was already shaped by these story elements and we simply assumed them as the normative way of being human and living with one another. In other words, we are all born into some kind of story that already exists, one that shapes us from the moment of our birth. Some describe this as a cultural story.[2]

Charles Taylor and Social Imaginaries

The Catholic philosopher Charles Taylor uses the term *social imaginary* to refer to the ways in which we are shaped by these basic kinds of stories that lie in the background of our lives like the props in a stage play.[3] He recognizes that often we seek to live out of a conscious set of values and principles that we articulate to one another.

For example, many Christians who are part of local churches are committed to the value of being a *community*. Indeed, the language and structures of church life seek to express and embody this voiced commitment to being a community. The word is often written into mission or values statements of a local church and then embodied in such things as small groups. At this conscious level where we articulate our convictions about life, it would seem that Christians are shaped by the value of community. Mark Lau Branson and the other Christians who formed the church in Oakland began to discover, however, that things just aren't that simple or straightforward.

Charles Taylor argues that behind such public expression of who we are lies another, more elusive but much more critical self-understanding. A social imaginary is about "the ways people imagine their social existence, how they fit together with others, how things go on between them and their fellows, the expectations that are normally met, and the deeper normative notions that underlie these expectations."[4] He is referring to the ways in which people imagine their social existence, the common understanding people have about the way things are supposed to work; social imaginaries are about how we make sense of our world. Social imaginaries create a taken-for-granted set of common assumptions about our normal expectations and common understandings around how things work and how we're supposed to act in the world. The social imaginary is "the largely unstructured and inarticulate understanding of our whole situation, within which particular features of our world show up for us in the sense we have."[5]

Mark Lau Branson and his friends in Oakland, while motivated by communitarian ideals of the New Testament, discovered that a whole other imagination was also at work. Mark described this other imagination as "consumerism . . . shaped by such priorities as individual choice, personal affectivity, and expectations (imaginations) that emphasized the pursuit of careers that should supply meaning and resources for our lives."[6]

Taylor describes a social imaginary in terms of what seems to us as just self-evident ways of living. This assumption of individualism is an example of a social imaginary. We don't go around claiming we are self-actualizing individuals. In fact we use the language of community with one another as Christians. We use this public discourse as if it actually shaped our lives when, in reality, a whole other "operating" system of individualism is at work determining our choices and actions.

In the parable of the three friends, in the way the missional conversation has been shaped in North America, we remain captive to a social imaginary that puts the church at the center of our focus and actions. Such a social imaginary misses what God is up to in the world in our day. All the talk about becoming externally driven or missional *churches* only intensifies a captivity to a social imaginary contrary to the movement of God.

Living in Language Houses

One of the primary ways a society or group carries forward their social imaginaries is through language.[7] Branson states it this way:

> A community's imagination, its stories and practices, its history and expectations—these are created and carried by words that interpret everything. We are constructed by and live our lives in and through language; not language as we have come to understand it as a tool, as positivism or propaganda, but more like a "house of language."[8]

Just as the house in which we live provides us with the symbols and basic elements that give identity, meaning, and the resources for our life (my home is set out in a certain pattern shaped around my needs and my perspective on what is important for thriving as a human being), so the ways we live, understand how the world works, and act inside social institutions (like the church) are shaped by this notion of a language house.[9]

But language is not simply a construction, something we build out of raw materials to suit our needs or place us in a shelter of meaning. Language isn't like inert brick or construction timber. It is far more! It is the house where our humanity is formed and continually made over; it gives expression to our deepest senses of who we are, the mystery of what it means to be human in a world that does not go on forever—where we create and die. Language is the realm of the poet, of desire and hope, of the search for and expression of infinity. Through language we search heaven and earth for meaning. Language is indispensable to being human. This is the reason stories recited from traditions or novels wrestling with aspects of our humanness are so important to us. Living in a house of language is at the heart of what makes us human.[10]

We do not live in a simple world comprised of a singular story about the meaning of the world. We all live in very complex houses of language, shaped out of multiple, competing stories about what it means to be human and what are the true sources of the self. It is naive in the extreme to believe that we have some clear access to the truth of the world that removes from us the problem of living in a multistory house filled with rooms and closets, passageways and alcoves, basements and attics filled with many conflicting stories that are continually shaping and reshaping our lives. Charles Taylor and Mark Lau Branson make it clear in their different accounts of social imaginaries and houses of language that we can be shaped by our ways of seeing the world that are largely out of our sight, even while we are articulating another set of beliefs.

Part two introduces a language house and social imaginary that is fundamentally different from the one described in the first part of this book, where the ecclesiocentric nature of the missional conversation was introduced. The language house of the churches in North America continues to make the church the center of its social imaginary even as it uses new words, such as *missional* and *emergent*. The captivity to this social imaginary goes deep. It is not amenable to simplistic techniques, such as becoming outwardly focused churches. Something far more radical and transformative is required. To get to what that might mean, we need to listen intently to another, very different language house and enter a radically different social imaginary. This journey takes us into the twin texts of the Gospel of Luke and the book of Acts.

PART 2

THE LANGUAGE HOUSE OF LUKE-ACTS

A NARRATIVE FOR SHAPING OUR TIME OF MISSIONAL FORMATION

4

Finding God in the Concrete

Locating Our Stories in the Here and Now

A language house predetermines how one sees the world or reads a text. We always bring our language house to the task of interpreting the world and understanding how to navigate our way. In part one I describe one way my own language house shaped the ways I interpreted Lesslie Newbigin and shaped the missional conversation as an element of ecclesiology. I was shaken by the recognition that I participated in writing a book on missional church, spoke at conferences on the subject, and was a core member of a missional network yet blind to my own captivity to this monologue. I lived inside a dominant story—the church as the subject and object of God's activities—that shaped the ways I read the biblical narratives and how I responded to my cultural contexts. While hard to accept, when I recognized this language house, most of the books about the missional church that I was now seeing were, for me, not just wrongheaded, but I came to believe they were fundamentally misdirecting the work of the church in North America.

We need a radically different language house and social imaginary if we are to reflect faithfully the nature of God's missional vocation in our context. A first step is the recognition that we're not in a three-way conversation but a monologue in which the *church* dominates, using the other conversation partners (the biblical narratives and our culture[s]) as objects in its visions, values, plans, strategies, and goals (we use the Bible to proof-text our vision statements and turn our contexts into objects of the ends of church growth, health, effectiveness, and so on). The power of this language house/social imaginary is evidenced in how a good many leaders actually celebrate the success of this monologue, assuming faithfulness to the gospel in our culture is synonymous with their church's vision, mission, and values statements. When I propose our captivity to an ecclesiocentric language house, such leaders sigh in frustration, asking with consternation: "What's the issue? Our values, vision, and mission statements are 'biblical,' and, besides, they work! How can you be against growth and success when our programs to get people into church and believing the gospel are so effective? Aren't we supposed to be growing the church? If we can use the best marketing practices to attract seekers and do things so that people feel their needs are being met as they come to church and join our worship, then aren't we effectively growing the kingdom?"

It's hard to argue against successful results in our culture! Nevertheless, this monologue is the furthest thing from a Christian imagination. It can only misdirect us as God's people when so much is being questioned about the motives of the organizations of our society. Recently a friend sent me an email describing his own wrestling with something he senses happening across North America. He said: "This will come as no surprise, of course, but I'm encountering more and more people who describe themselves as being 'between congregations,' without giving much indication that they're eager or hopeful about finding a church in which to pitch their tents. I think 'Christian but not churched' is the rapidly emerging 'spiritual but not religious' for our time—and the ones I talk to about this are often those who are most, not least, serious about their faith. They read, think, practice spiritual disciplines and works of service and justice, but don't 'go' anywhere. And if my anecdotal conversations with a variety of people in recent days is any indication, this isn't a trickle; it's a torrent."

This is like the canary in the mine, the early warning system that the language houses of our churches with their ecclesiocentric focus on their own growth and values are no longer able to hold the imagination or passions of more and more people who identify themselves as Christians. We need a radically different language house.

When I talk about this concern with church leaders, I get blank looks. Speaking at a conference for young leaders, I began by saying we wouldn't talk about the church during our time together. I indicated that I wouldn't be responding to questions about the church. The response was stunning! These young leaders, in their twenties and thirties, were angry with me for most of the first day. They shouted, stormed out to caucus, came back in, and argued with me about changing the agenda. I didn't!

For a time I doubted myself, becoming discouraged by their fierce responses. I was challenging and disrupting their language houses. The next day, however, some began to catch on to what I was up to. The focus of conversation shifted; they were talking together about the meaning of the gospel amid the varied cultures they lived in. Those were wonderful conversations as more and more of these young leaders started to engage the gospel stories in ways they had never imagined before. On the last day we returned to the church question, but now their responses were very different because they had been invited into another language house for a brief period of time. They were now struggling and wondering if the leaders of the local churches to which they were returning could ever get the shift in imagination and thinking they had just experienced.

My desire is to shape a conversation that attends to the biblical engagement in the shifting cultural settings in which we find ourselves. The issue is not about being for or against the church—that is a nonsensical choice. I am utterly for the church in all its ordinariness and localness. I am arguing for a different starting point, a different language house so we can understand and practice what it means to be God's missionary people.

One of the primary ways we can discover and be invited into a different language house is by reconnecting with the social imaginaries that are being constructed in the biblical narratives. In this part we will focus on the writing of Luke in both the Gospel and the book of Acts.

Bible and Story

Scripture is filled with amazing stories that go to the heart of the issues we're facing in our crazy, pluralist, consumer-driven cultures focused on self-actualizing individuals living in instrumental relationships (in which people relate to each other out of roles or what each can get from the other). In Vancouver, where I live, there is no longer a majority ethnic group. A hundred years ago Scottish Presbyterians and Chinese workers formed the city, which included British citizens, those from other parts of Europe, and native peoples who were largely considered not a part of the citizenry.

Europeans (Scots/English) were in charge, setting the rules, while the Chinese kept their heads low, and the native peoples were hidden. Today all of that has been swept away in a radically new cultural mosaic in which Chinese descendants are the ascendant majority with growing segments of Iranians, Russians, Sikhs, and peoples from every part of the globe.

Christians in Vancouver can no longer read the story of the good Samaritan as a nice, sentimental moral story about caring for people across the street or at the rescue mission who are like them but less fortunate. They cannot hear the question, Who is my neighbor? without the disruptive awareness that *neighbor* now means another who has not been a part of their language house. In this story of the stranger who stops beside the road to care for a Jew, Jesus was challenging the language house of his own people, which clearly delineated who was accepted and who wasn't, who was in and who was out. This parable is a radical deconstruction of their language house, and the fierce opposition toward him is an illustration of how hard it is for any group of people to have their language house deconstructed. The response is resistance and accusations of betrayal or ignorance. In that story the language house of a group of Christians (in Vancouver that of a European, ethnotribal church) who have assumed they were dominant is radically decentered. You can't go to a monocultural church in this kind of city and even begin to imagine you can hear the gospel.

This struggle to engage and transform language houses runs through so many of Jesus's encounters in the Gospel of Luke. When the disciples see others healing and claiming to do this in the name of Jesus or observe a town refusing hospitality to Jesus, they seek permission to deal with these matters out of their current social imaginary of what God was up to in Jesus (they want to bring judgment and destruction on the people involved). Jesus's response shows the extent to which their language houses needed to be deconstructed before they could enter into the future Jesus was forming.

Jesus sought to address these language houses as a storyteller. His stories were about what ordinary people were doing in their ordinary lives. They were about farmers building barns, women cleaning houses, people injured on roadways being attended to by strangers, tiny grains growing into huge plants, businessmen making profits, young radicals ready to give away all their upper-class privileges until it was time to actually take the plunge, and so on. The Gospel writers took these stories and put them together to tell their own stories of what Jesus was doing and how the good news of God's in-breaking future was affecting the cultures in which these early Christians lived. To recover the conversation between the biblical narratives and a radical engagement with our culture(s), we need to understand something of how these early Christians saw themselves in relationship to the larger story of God's actions in their world.

A Continuing Conversation

The early Christians to whom Matthew, Mark, Luke, and John were writing their Gospels understood they were part of something that did not begin with Jesus or at Pentecost. They knew they had been brought inside a bigger story, one that began long before they came onto the scene. The Gospels were, in fact, part of a continuing conversation; they were written from within powerful memories. From the beginning of Luke's Gospel, for example, there is direct and indirect allusion to the Jewish Scriptures and the promises of God. It's impossible to understand the aim of any of the Gospel writers without this awareness of the larger narrative that shaped them. What Luke, for example, does with Old Testament narratives about God's promised future and how it is being worked out in Jesus represents, as we shall see, a radical reinterpretation of how texts had come to be understood. In other words, Luke was seeking to reconstruct the language houses of these early communities in the light of Jesus and the unfolding events these early Christians needed to navigate.

The ways local churches would take form and understand their place in these cultures was not in their being Platonic, ideal churches with well-crafted vision and values and mission statements, but through the existential wrestling with the story of Jesus in these shifting local contexts. Luke's crafting of the stories in his Gospel and in Acts can't be understood as saying, "Just go and be Jesus in your culture." This is pure romanticism. Luke illustrates how this early church was wrestling mightily with its tradition and the social contexts in which these young Christians were living at the end of the first century. Again, questions about the church—its shape, order, forms, and mission—come out of this primary wrestling. Those who make the missional question about the church miss this and thus continually fall into the ecclesiocentric trap.

We will discover, in fact, that by the end of the first century many Christians were struggling with the language house they had created to explain the Christian story. There was a massive amount of confusion and anxiety among these young, struggling communities of Gentile Christians spread across the fringes and centers of the Roman Empire. The language house they had been given to make sense of the stories of Jesus and the birth of the church simply didn't make sense of their experience. Things hadn't turned out as promised or expected. People were wondering what had gone wrong. Luke turns to his project of writing for Theophilus to retheologize the story of Jesus's coming in the light of failed expectations. He intended to create a new language house.

It is this kind of journey that the churches of North America must again embark on if they are to discover the ways of God in a world that no longer seems to fit the plans and expectations written into their mission, vision, and values statements. Those making this journey must understand how radical the transformation of imagination is that is demanded. It is a journey that moves from a primary focus on the church to the place of making the church work again in the neighborhoods and communities where we live so we can ask what God is already doing ahead of us in these ordinary places.

Discovering the Concreteness of the Ordinary

Luke crafts a story to help Gentile Christians find the language and imagination that would reorient their understanding of what God was doing in the world and, therefore, who they were to be in their community. As we shall see, he addresses people's questions about what had gone wrong by giving them a different social imaginary.

He presents a language house that gives a theological and contextual description of what God was up to in the world through Jesus. He achieves this by reframing the story in terms of a missionary God continually calling people to go on disruptive, unthinkable, risky journeys for the sake of the kingdom. This is the story I want to look at in this part.

The One revealed in Jesus, if Luke is to be trusted, addresses us over and over again through particular, concrete dealings with a people, Israel. In the concreteness of the stories of these people, God is known. Likewise, in Jesus, we learn that we can encounter this God only by listening in on the specific, concrete narratives of ordinary people in little communities we come to call the *ecclesia*.

We don't encounter this God through universal principles, formulas, visions, and values but through the concrete, grounded stories of God's life in the ordinary. Luke takes pains, for example, to locate Jesus's birth in the concreteness of place at a specific time to particular people with names and addresses. Only through his indwelling place and time is this God known. Luke's Gospel, and his account of Jesus's birth story, begins in this way:

> Many have undertaken to draw up an account of the things that have been fulfilled among us, just as they were handed down to us by those who from the first were eyewitnesses and servants of the word. Therefore, since I myself have carefully investigated everything from the beginning, it seemed good also to me to write an orderly account for you, most excellent Theophilus so that you may know the certainty of the things you have been taught.
>
> Luke 1:1–4

These brief sentences are Luke's equivalent of a marketing announcement for a book launch telling people what it's all about. Luke is going to retell a narrative. He will give an account, choose events, organize a trajectory to tell the people that, out of all the stories competing for ascendancy and control over them, this is the one they can commit themselves to, because, unlike all the other stories, this is God's story.

This is a tall order for Luke, because already many of these young communities of the gospel are wondering about the story they've taken up and suspect that it may not be as clear and trustworthy as they were led to believe.

We should make no mistake about what Luke is up to here. He has to address the language house of diverse Gentile communities who are struggling with the story they have received, which just doesn't seem to cohere any longer. Luke is determined to convince them that in the midst of a world of competing narratives, this is the one about Jesus and the good news of God that is worth giving their lives to because it is God's. But the stories he will tell, stories of conflict with neighbors, stories of widows and ordinary people, will turn expected ways upside down. In the language house of their expectations, they will make no sense.

The beginning sentences of the Gospel have the character of stubborn fact about them. Eyewitnesses handed down the story. This story is rooted in events; things took place that needed recording for someone who required certainty after hearing it from others. Can it be true? Is this something one can believe? Even then, right at the beginning, despite the eyewitnesses, it was still amazingly strange that these events could be true.

Today, however, the strangeness is that we continue to read these narratives through language houses that are primarily about meeting our needs and shaping our own self-actualization. We have a whole language house about what the Christian story is intended to do. I am aware of how often over the past year I have listened to sermons and religious leaders turn the biblical narratives into a useful handbook for making one's life work more successful. I'm aware of how this Oprahization of the Christian narrative has turned us ever more quickly into anxiety-laden, functional atheists needing ways to use God to make our lives work. We seem to have become more and more Peter Pan–like, driven by childlike expectations that if we just close our eyes, imagine what we want, and believe God has this for us, then Jesus will help us have the better future we want to create for ourselves.

This way of hearing the narratives of the Bible has come to be called "spirituality"—an indulgent process of imagining that betrays the language house in which we live. Gurus, like Tolle Eckhart, have instinctively concluded that if the dominant narrative is all about the self and its fulfillment, you don't need this religious stuff about God and Jesus. Why carry the religious baggage when you can do it for yourself? Eckhart is only pursuing what is already the functional atheism in the language house of our churches, the make-yourself-better-through-positive-thinking-and-vitamins crowd.

Luke has a radically different agenda because he understands that God has something in mind that is far more expansive than self-fulfillment. And this agenda of constructing a new language house will involve engagement with the concrete ordinariness of the local.

We know God in the concreteness of particular stories that have occurred at specific times and places. We come to know the nature of the gospel, not through some form of romantic universalizing, but in the social constructions of our lives, through the social imaginaries of our time and place, and through the concrete encounters we have with the people and communities about us.[1]

5

Texts That Propose a World

Discovering a Different Way to Enter Scripture

The Scriptures propose a world to us. They invite us into a way of reading and understanding who we are as human beings, our ends, and the intentions of God.[1] This idea of Scripture proposing a world may seem like a strange idea to us at first. What does it mean?

Currently I am reading a new biography of Samuel Johnson, written in celebration of the three hundredth anniversary of his birth.[2] The book begins in Johnson's birthplace of Litchfield near Birmingham, England. The careful research of the author, Peter Martin, takes you into the world of Johnson and this small town at the beginning of the eighteenth century. One only has to read a little to recognize that Johnson lived in a radically different world from the one any of us reading this book live in. To come near to Johnson, one must be ready to work at entering his world as much as possible.

My wife is reading the novel *The Elegance of the Hedgehog*.[3] She is so drawn into the story of the women who inhabit a world shaped around a small Parisian apartment building that she will actually read me sections. The author invites the reader to reflect on his or her life through the lens of lives that seem without meaning. Into this world comes a Japanese man who will turn the managed lives of the people in the novel upside down.

I am also reading *The Fourth Part of the World: The Race to the Ends of the Earth and the Epic Story of the Map That Gave America Its Name*.[4] It is about sixteenth-century explorations that led to the creation of the map that gave this continent the name the Americas. Reading this book is like being led by its author into a world nothing like ours, not just in terms of life habits or practices but in terms of its assumptions about how the world worked and the place of human beings in it.

Each book illustrates the fact that human beings live in worlds. Walter Brueggemann makes the same point in terms of biblical texts. Writing about our own time, the world in which we live as Western, North American people at the beginning of the twenty-first century, he states, "The core of our new awareness is that the world we have taken for granted in economics, politics, and elsewhere is an imaginative construal. And if it is a construal, then from any other perspective, the world can yet be construed differently."[5] He goes on to propose that the biblical texts present to us a counterimagination. He suggests that if we are willing to listen long and hard enough, what emerges from the biblical texts is a different world. Then he makes clear his own conviction about this listening and attending: "The *proposed world* offered in the text runs dead against my *presumed world*."[6]

The first part of this book described a specific aspect of the North American Christian "world" that is massively problematic to the project of being God's people. In this part we are seeking to enter and listen in on the world Luke was describing for Gentile Christians across the empire for whom the Christian story was no longer making sense. Luke proposed to them a world and in so doing sought to reshape their language house. He wanted to re-form their social imaginaries to help them grasp again the nature of God's actions in the world.

Colin Greene and Martin Robinson describe Scripture as texts that create a world, "opening before us a host of imaginative possibilities" for reconfiguring our own language house. They ask how we can "actually learn to indwell the story and so find ourselves within the world that the text opens up before us."[7] The point they make is that wherever the church learns to reenact the world that Scripture opens before us, "a fundamental reconfiguration takes place that creates a new world, a new history, a new possibility of fresh adventures, a new imagined opportunity."[8]

A World Proposed in the Concreteness of the Ordinary

The world proposed in Scripture is about a way of being in the world that attends to the concreteness of everyday life rather than romanticized idealizations of what the church or a culture ought to be. Scripture roots us, physically and materially, in, for, with, alongside, and at times against the ordinary people in our communities. The world the biblical texts propose is not about the selling or marketing of a product but the re-forming of a world in the midst of the ordinary.

The Johannine prologue isn't some neo-Romantic ideal when it describes the coming of God into the world in terms of "pitching tent" beside us, or, in a more colloquial interpretation, moving right into the neighborhood. This is the re-presenting of a world in which the God of Scripture is known in the ordinary and everyday. The Bible is not a book of ethics filled with rules and guidelines about how to live effective lives. It is not the rulebook from which we extract the right vision and values we then apply like a template in our time. It is not an ancient *Chicken Soup for the Soul* or *Seven Habits of Highly Effective People*. It doesn't invite us to find personal, psychological guidelines for living. On the contrary, the Scriptures challenge and turn upside down some of the most basic and cherished assumptions we have about what God is doing in the world.

If the biblical texts propose a world that reads and deconstructs the language houses we have created to manage our world, it does this by calling us back to the local and ordinary. In terms of the relationship between gospel, church, and culture that has shaped the missional conversation, this perspective of locality and ordinariness is critical. What besets the North American church, even in some of the new proposals being offered to make it missional, is a pervasive romanticizing of the church or an idealism that believes we must frame the "true" church in its "intended" forms before we can function properly as the people of God.

It is in this context that leaders labor over mission, vision, and values statements. These documents are not shaped by the world of the biblical texts but more by eighteenth-century Romanticism and pre-Christian Platonism. This point can be illustrated by Raphael's sixteenth-century painting *The School of Athens*.[9] The center of the fresco depicts Plato (on the left) and Aristotle (on the right). Plato is pointing upward toward the heavens and Aristotle downward toward the ground. Their bodily expressions communicate several interpretations to the painting. At one level one could imagine the Renaissance artist wanting to express a certain kind of symmetry that gives due place to both the philosophic worlds these two great thinkers represent. Each is holding a bound, leather copy of his own writing, Plato, *Timaeus*; Aristotle, *Nicomachean Ethics*. Yet we see that Aristotle, looking younger and more vigorous than his mentor, is standing slightly forward of Plato, signifying a place in the emerging understanding of sixteenth-century European thought.

The two men represent two differing worlds, two opposing readings of how to understand and interpret the world. Plato, in pointing up toward the heavens, is indicating that truth is to be found outside this world in the forms, the ideal types, which, when known, can then be brought down to earth so that the world can be ordered after the true forms in the heavens. In contrast, Aristotle points down to the earth, emphasizing that the world is known in the practical, concrete particularity and ordinariness of the everyday.

These figures are a powerful image of a basic struggle that continues to permeate the imagination of Christian leaders into the twenty-first century. Part one of this book has argued that the language house of the church, in terms of its own ecclesiocentricity, including its notions of leadership and planning, is fundamentally Platonic in nature. It further argued that this idealism has created a language house that continues to misguide and misdirect almost all attempts in North America to address the missiological question raised by Lesslie Newbigin more than a quarter century ago, namely, What is the nature of a missionary engagement with that cultural complex we have come to know as late-modern culture in the West?

Part two is proposing that the biblical texts invite us into a radically different language world than that represented by the figure of Plato in Raphael's fresco. The biblical texts depict a world much more like that of the Aristotle figure, who, with hand pointing to the "earthbound" nature of our reality, suggests that we know and discover only as we are deeply engaged in the local, ordinary, and concrete particulars of place and time. The world construed by the biblical texts tells us that this is the only place where we can encounter the God who has come to us in Jesus Christ. We shall see that Luke, in the Gospel and Acts, is reframing a world that we must rediscover if we are to form communities of the gospel in our time.

Dwelling within Biblical Texts

For those of us trained in a modern seminary context, engaging Scripture involves mastering texts through the use of grammatical, syntactical, and language tools. These are, and will continue to be, important hermeneutical tools for everyone involved in Christian ministry. But if we are to follow the wisdom of such brilliant biblical interpreters (men and women skilled in the use of the tools named above) as Walter Brueggemann, then these methods are neither sufficient nor primary. Letting the biblical texts re-form our language house is not primarily about abstracting principles that are then applied, in some claimed objective form, to our current situation. Something radically different is required.

We are invited inside the biblical texts not as miners crushing rock to extract its essential minerals but as travelers ready to be surprised in ways that unfold the unspoken assumptions in our stories, calling them into question in ways that disorient us so that our stories of what God is doing might be transformed.

We are people formed inside a specific kind of language house. When we come to Scripture, we do not come from nowhere but from particular somewheres. We are, for example, those who live deeply inside the narratives of late modernity; we are shaped by the narratives of consumerism and individualism; we expect that with the right formulas we can make the world work for us in our own chosen ways. All of these are stories already deep within us, continually determining how we read the world and what we believe about how to be Christians.

Our underlying story remains that of power and control; it is the story of how we, as human beings, wrestled from the world the keys to the mansion of knowledge and understanding so that we could open all the doors, go in, and get for ourselves everything inside. Our narrative is still about being in control. This is the reason we create measures and metrics and demographics and so on—we believe that control is the answer to almost every question we have as human beings. We are convinced that we can get the skills and training we need to be in control of environments and texts to get what we want. Inside this story we remain unchallenged and unchanged, living in the illusion that we make the world according to our own powers. This is how we approach the biblical stories. They are to be mined for our own purposes.

Scripture invites us into a radically different world. Jesus turns to two inquisitive men and says, "Come and see" (John 1:39); in so doing, like Alice in Wonderland, they hurtle down a hole into a topsy-turvy world where they have little or no control. In Jesus's world we enter a story that turns upside down the ways we have understood our world and ourselves. It is as if these stories are about a counterintuitive way of life that, at first, makes little sense.

> "But I don't want to go among mad people," Alice remarked.
>
> "Oh, you can't help that," said the Cat. "We're all mad here. I'm mad. You're mad."
>
> "How do you know I'm mad?" said Alice.
>
> "You must be," said the Cat, "or you wouldn't have come here."[10]

To understand what God is about in the world, we must enter texts that will not be mastered and controlled. In the Old Testament there are texts describing a people who become continually a question to themselves. They struggle with what it means to be inside God's story, while they have to live in the midst of all the other stories around them, demanding attention, offering order, control, and security.

Jacob must wrestle with God all night. In the end he can only participate in God's story as he is wounded; he must limp for the rest of his life. But the man, Jacob, receives a new name, Israel, meaning *he who strives with God*. This was Israel's experience of being inside God's story, as it must be for all who are drawn to it.

Why would it be any different for us? We are those schooled to believe we already *have* the story; we are in control of the text and so we know the world configured by the Bible. But the stories of God's engagements with us are not propositions and truths we can, with enough study and training, master (many of us are, after all, masters of divinity). We have been schooled to stand at a distance from the story, outside, as trained observers looking down from above. But these stories cannot be known in this way. Those who enter them will have their language houses turned upside down.

The Way of Jesus

Jesus's stories came out of his listening to and comprehending what was happening among people with whom he lived. One imagines that for many years as a carpenter he watched and listened with the eyes and ears of someone who loved the people around him. He sought to know them, not turn them into the objects of his plans. One suspects that's the reason his stories were so powerful. He did not turn people into objects he would use to achieve his goals. Rather, his stories invited people to let the drama of God's working among them impact their own stories.

But I have to keep emphasizing this over and over again—it is too important to miss—he didn't do this to make them objects of some new church. He was inviting them into the adventure of God's story because this is where life is discovered.

There was this freedom in Jesus's stories. I can't believe those who heard them felt that Jesus had some other agenda going on underneath, that he was only interested in how they could fit into his plan. In Jesus's hands, stories opened worlds for people whose imaginations had collapsed down narrow tunnels with little light. Often Jesus's stories became landmines. At first, they seemed innocent enough, but once a person got inside the story or parable, it would explode unexpectedly, crack open little worlds, disorient a taken-for-granted life, disrupt practiced scenarios, and overturn assumptions so that the brightness of God's future could be seen.

Scripture is full of these stories that chronicle God's everyday dealings with ordinary people. Scripture isn't a textbook of information or moral direction; it isn't a formula for making life work or a religious Dr. Phil handbook for people who want to improve their lives, expand their bottom line, or ensure their kids get the right start in life. It is full of stories that invite us into the drama of where God is moving creation. Christians are invited to embody this drama.[11]

Performing Scripture

Christopher Lash uses a helpful word to capture what this kind of Christian life is about. The word he uses is *performance*. Here's the way he illustrates what this means. To experience a Beethoven symphony or Shakespearean tragedy, it's not sufficient—if we are to enter the drama of the music or the play—merely to read notes or memorize lines. While important, it's not enough just to read the historical background of the works or absorb the evaluations of music or drama critics. At the heart of engaging Beethoven or Shakespeare is the *performance* of the score and the play—you need to experience a symphony or a theater group actually *performing* it. Only in the performance do Beethoven's music and Shakespeare's plays assume life.

When my wife, Jane, was the principal of a private school in downtown Toronto, our three children, Paul, Sara Jane, and Aaron, were students there. Very early on, from about grade 6, Jane would introduce Shakespeare to her English classes. They would read the play together. Then during the summer at Shakespeare in the Park, a professional theater group would perform Shakespeare's plays. We would pack a picnic supper (it was more like a major five-star meal, truth be told), call some friends, and head for the park with blankets. We'd find a great spot in the large bowl-like natural amphitheater in the woods, eat supper as a gang, and await the beginning of something wonderful, like *A Midsummer Night's Dream*, presented under the stars in the middle of the city. This was our chance to engage in the *performance* of the play. To this day, our kids can enter those plays with joy and energy because they didn't simply read the play in a classroom; they entered the play through its performance.

In a similar way, Scripture can only really be engaged as it is performed within a community of God's people. Don't jump to conclusions here! I'm not back into the old church questions; I'm not doing the very thing I've spent so much time saying is the wrong direction. I'm going to argue that one of the most critical ways of *performing* Scripture and entering the world of God's story today is by discovering how to perform together the world that Luke unfolds to the Gentile Christians he is addressing.

The Gospels are written to help diverse and rapidly changing groups of house churches spreading throughout the empire make sense of what is happening to them. Luke-Acts tells a lot of the same stories as Matthew and Mark, but Luke tells them in different ways as he engages young churches in situations for which they have little experience or preparation. Luke's stories are drawn from "all that Jesus began to do and teach" (Acts 1:1). They're an account of things eyewitnesses had handed down (see Luke 1:1–2). Luke provides a type of chronology of what had been happening. But he also wrote his two volumes to address house churches struggling with huge questions about their identity and future. They needed help to understand what had happened to the first generation of Christians and why so much had changed. Luke's stories invited these second-generation Christians into an understanding of what had taken place that would help them confidently *perform* the gospel in their own context.

6

Shifting Worlds

The Need for a New Text

Luke wrote his two-volume work toward the end of the first century. It addresses small, dispersed communities of Gentile Christians who found themselves in a radically different situation than that described in the early chapters of Acts after Pentecost and the outward missionary impulse of Paul and others. The world had changed dramatically in the intervening years. Time had passed. Now Luke is engaging a second generation of Christians for whom the founding stories were secondhand.

Little clusters of household churches in what is now modern-day Turkey were confused about the Christian story they had received. They needed some fundamental reorientation in terms of the gospel and what God was doing in the world. The assumptions that had shaped their embrace of and commitment to the Christian story had been undermined. They felt at odds with a lot of what they'd assumed the gospel was about and would accomplish in a brief period of time.

One is drawn to these texts because they describe a situation not dissimilar to our own. It seems that at different times in the life of the church, particular texts stand out like guideposts pointing the way for its life; these texts are like barometers that show the temperament and environment of the church at a given time. From the late nineteenth century right up to the latter part of the twentieth, it seemed that the paradigmatic text for Christians in the United Kingdom and North America was that of Jesus's charge to the disciples in Matthew, otherwise known as the Great Commission:

> All authority in heaven and on earth has been given to me. Therefore go and make disciples of all nations, baptizing them in the name of the Father and of the Son and of the Holy Spirit, and teaching them to obey everything I have commanded you. And surely I am with you always, to the very end of the age.
>
> Matthew 28:18–20

The lines are inscribed into the memory of almost anyone who attended a Sunday school or had even a passing acquaintance with a church. Huge missionary movements and conferences (such as Urbana in North America) were built around the robust, muscular sense of call and destiny built into the interpretation and proclamation of this text in the last century.

The social context of the church from the mid-nineteenth century well into the latter part of the twentieth was the expansion of the West in terms of its civilizing and Christianizing moves across the world. The mantle of empire first belonged to the British with their Victorian-era sense of Christian destiny. It was on the back of this powerful narrative of empire, of European civilization with its economic and military might, that the outward movement of the church took place. The rallying text that captured this movement of God and country was Matthew 28:19–20 with its command to go out to all the world and make disciples.

By the midpoint of the last century this mantle of empire and Christian destiny had moved from the United Kingdom to America, but Matthew 28 continued to be the text that galvanized Christians to action, shaping their sense of call and fueling a truly amazing output of missionary energies around the world. In many ways this bold, muscular, manifest-destiny form of Christian life in the West had as its underpinnings the sense that the West would be dominant in the history of the world and the purposes of God. There was a powerful sense of being in control of the world—for good, honorable, and God-given reasons. And in a parallel way, there was a strong sense of being in the current of God's purposes, as understood and interpreted in Matthew 28.

The environment has changed so dramatically over the past twenty or thirty years that the sense of a special, privileged place in the world is being questioned. The conviction that God has special purposes for the West, first Britain and then America, is quickly eroding so that we carry about this awkward sense that our picture of who we've been as Christians no longer fits the reality of the world in which we live. Confidence in our identity and vocation as Christians in the West has weakened in a postcolonial world. The emergence of a new, globalizing world in which a multiplicity of cultural narratives vie for place has come about with such rapidity that we don't know how to make sense of it. After the fall of Communism, when the final ascent of the West had been achieved, we were supposed to be living in the end of history.

All of this has proved to be a chimera as political and economic power seems to be shifting elsewhere and religious pluralism and multiple fundamentalisms take center stage. The economic meltdown and a "jobless" recovery leave many confused about what happened to the dominant story of manifest destiny and a nation under God. Few imagined this kind of world at the beginning of the last quarter of the twentieth century.[1] It no longer feels like the confident era of the West when it was so simple to define Christian identity in terms of Matthew 28 and know that pretty much everyone understood and agreed with this robust confidence in Western Christianity.

We find ourselves as Western Christians in a place where we are no longer sure of our identity, no longer sure of where we fit into the overall scheme of history or the unfolding purposes of God. The increasing sense that the mantle of Christian vitality and mission has been removed from the West, that the energy of Christian meaning and future now lies in the southern hemisphere, all of this is creating a different ethos among Christians in the West in which we are less and less sure of ourselves and feel less and less able to articulate with confidence the nature of our call.

One result of this anxiety about our identity and the meaning of the gospel has been the turning of Christian life into little more than private personal experience—going to church and attracting other people to our church. At the same time many Christians are experiencing anxiety because the Christian narrative seems less and less connected to people's growing sense of economic, social, environmental, and spiritual dislocation.

In such a context there is a struggle to articulate what it might mean to live the gospel. What starts to emerge is that the paradigmatic nature of Matthew 28 in the social, economic, and geopolitical framing of the last century and a half may no longer have the capacity to frame a Christian imagination in this new space. The language house of empire, power, and control with which Matthew 28 has been invested is an imaginary that can no longer provide us with the resources to understand what Christian life and witness might be in this new place. This is not to denigrate or deny the ongoing vocation of mission in the world. It is to ask some basic questions about the ways in which we will need to let the biblical texts read us in our new situation. The proposition being made in this part is that Luke's engagements with these second-generation Christians can provide us with the language house we need to reframe our own situation and reimagine the nature of Christian life in the West.

Addressing a Whole New Reality

Those second-generation churches to whom Luke wrote were facing a crisis of meaning because, as we will see below, many of the assumptions they had made about the direction of the Christian movement had not come about. Luke is seeking to reorient the thinking and imagination of these Christians.

Our situation in North America today can be seen as very similar. For many of us the promises and expectations of the gospel seem to have failed. Just as Luke does not offer the Gentile Christians forms of adjustment, so our own crisis of meaning as Christians will not be addressed with one more set of tactics. Much of what is being offered today as "missional" are tactics for making the church more successful or effective. There is, for example, a good deal of talk about becoming "externally focused" churches. But this is merely a new tactic to make the church work again. The challenge facing Christian life today in North America is not going to be addressed by switching focus from some "inside" to "outside" engagements. The crisis of the North American church is about its language house (where the conversations are directed and where they are not directed).

Something more fundamental than new tactics to make the church effective is required. Many church leaders still find this hard to accept. They assume their understanding of the gospel is perfectly in order and are, therefore, not open to hearing what Luke has to say, namely, that the need of our time is to allow the story of what God is doing in the world to re-form us all over again in a different way. Asking church questions and developing new "missional" church tactics will not address this.

These Gentile Christians for whom Luke wrote were invited to discover that the gospel wasn't a finished conversation, that, indeed, their language house was preventing them from perceiving what God was doing in the world. In our own time, the church is again filled with leaders who assume they already know what the gospel is all about. It's all been worked out ahead of time in their seminary training; they have written and passed denominational exams or completed fill-in-the-blanks church-planting workbooks. The thought that the biblical texts might propose to us another world within which we might need to re-form our understanding of the gospel sounds like nonsense or heresy. It feels like being placed on the edge of a slippery precipice where everything solid is changed into air. But we must go there! Unless, as leaders, we are willing to enter this in-between space that disrupts our settled assumptions and threatens our formulas and expectations, we will remain locked into a monologue of church questions and strategies.

I don't want to be misunderstood. At worship when I stand to say the Apostles' Creed, I'm confessing what I believe most deeply; when I kneel to receive the Eucharist, I'm confessing that here in the bread and wine is the food that gives us life. I am not saying that the church is unimportant or irrelevant! The argument I am making is that we have shaped the gospel in our churches around a whole set of cultural assumptions that we don't even recognize anymore—we need to have our worlds turned upside down before we'll become any good again as God's witnessing communities.

Luke's stories are like mines exploding in the middle of assumptions about the nature of the gospel and the location of Christian life. He proposes a way of understanding what God is about in the world that can invite us back into the trialogue Lesslie Newbigin was continually involved with and kept pointing us toward. The next chapters will examine the context and crisis that was faced by these second-generation Christians and why Luke needed to retell the gospel narratives in a way that retheologized the purposes of God in a confusing world. Then we will look at the specific ways Luke did this retheologizing in the early sections of Acts and we'll look at one specific text in the Gospel, Luke 10:1–12, to understand how he addressed the questions of these Christians concerning the way to know what God was up to in the world and what, therefore, it means to be the church.

A Pastor's Epiphany

A pastor, Tom, was trying to understand how he was perceived as a leader in a congregation in the American South. Tom was interviewing a series of people in the congregation as well as other ministry peers in the area. About twenty-five people had completed a questionnaire about him, and he wanted to discuss their responses concerning specific areas of his leadership. Here's a synopsis of Tom's report on one of those phone interviews:

"As we began the interview I thanked [the interviewee] for being willing to complete the questionnaire and now provide some further feedback on what the overall report was saying about some of my leadership skills and capacities. I explained to her again that these skills and capacities were not the ones we would usually associate with pastoral leadership (preaching, teaching, visitation, counseling, and so on) but were about the ability to lead a group of people through significant adaptive change within processes that were bottom-up rather than top-down. A long silence issued from the other end of the line. My anxiety grew. The person I was interviewing was a member of our congregation. She was now a seminary student and was serving as a Sunday school teacher as well as a volunteer for a program that reached into the community. The silence continued. I waited!

"'From what I've seen,' she said finally, 'the church is *closed* to the community. We push the annual denominational missions offering. To some extent we push Samaritan's Purse. But when it comes to a local child in the community, we're less likely to help.' She added, 'I visit a lot of the churches in this area through my volunteer work, I think ours, like most, is self-absorbed.'

"I found myself growing defensive. 'What about our visitation ministry?' I asked. Did this not suggest some interest in connecting with the people of our community?

"'This church is comfortable visiting people on the Sunday school list who haven't attended church recently,' she replied, 'but they're not really open to people in the community unless they're just like them.'"

Tom was not ready for this feedback, but, as he listened, he knew this young woman was telling the truth about the church. It was turned in on itself and the people related to those outside their church only if they were like them or interested in becoming like them by joining with them. This was the narrative of Tom's congregation. They were preoccupied with church questions, wondering how they could increase attendance and reach "seekers."

In this experience Tom had encountered the deep concern of most churches in North America: getting others to come to them and be a part of their lives. The monologue remains powerfully present, but in Luke 10 a different story and a different imagination are at work.

7

The Context and Crisis

The Shattered Hopes of Luke's Readers

David Bosch states that Luke had a crisis situation in mind when he set out to write his two-volume work. Gentile Christian communities spread out across the northeastern parts of the Roman Empire faced a crisis of identity. They were asking fundamental questions about who they were and what it meant to live as Christians in the midst of this empire.[1] Bosch saw this crisis emerging toward the end of the first century. It was characterized by a fundamental questioning of the nature of God's mission in the world, the meaning of what had been taken for granted as the self-evident nature of the gospel, and unfulfilled eschatological hope.

These concerns compelled Luke to write his two volumes, not primarily as a piece of straightforward historiography (which might be construed from the introduction he writes to Theophilus in the Gospel), but as the telling of history to address questions and reframe assumptions about the nature and purpose of these nascent communities of Jesus.[2] What then was the context and what were the sources of the crisis that caused Luke to write these two volumes?

A Perilous Minority

Theologian Barry Harvey describes part of the crisis among these early Christians in this way:

> During the first three centuries of church history, the followers of Christ constituted a minority in a world that viewed them with suspicion. The Romans widely regarded them as self-righteous and fanatical, worshipers of a capricious deity, atheists, the enemy of humankind and of a just social order. . . . Rome classified this new movement as a political society primarily because its adherents regarded it as fundamental that their allegiance to Christ cut across any allegiance to Caesar.[3]

These were people trying to work out the meaning of their existence in a time when the imperial power was demanding their allegiance. As we shall see, the first disciples of Jesus (especially those centered around Jerusalem) had specific expectations of how the gospel would engage the empires of the world. These expectations had not materialized. Gentile Christians found themselves in political and social contexts radically different from that of the movement's founders—those first-generation apostles and prophets were all dead and their understanding of how the gospel would work itself out in the world had been swept away after the fall of Jerusalem in AD 70.

A friend sent me a paper summarizing the work of a group of Canadian leaders in a denomination addressing the question, *How does this denomination understand and live out its missional identity in Canada at the dawn of the twenty-first century?* I wondered what kind of narrative they would weave in imagining how we might answer this question in Canada, because it is much, much further down the road of secularization than the United States. The Christian story is now a small, insignificant sideshow in Canada. The churches in this postmodern country face a profound crisis of identity.

The paper began with a discussion about the meaning of the word *ecclesia*, using biblical citations and the Greco-Roman cultural context to develop a certain kind of definition. Next, with the right definition set in place as a control mechanism, it engaged a series of books and resources on the theme of missional church to develop a series of *characteristics* of a missional church. This method, while recognizing the crisis, illustrates an ongoing captivity to the language house of modernity and, therefore, to the monologue of the church with both culture(s) and Scripture. They began with an abstract discussion of meanings, definitions, and characteristics of the *church*. The church, therefore, remained the beginning place, the focus, and the issue.

It seemed these leaders believed, if they could get the church question right, the rest would follow. But by asking the church question first, the questions of what God might be doing in the world and how the biblical narratives might reconfigure our imagination became subsets of church questions. The assumption of those who wrote the paper is that, once they'd developed the right definitions and established the right list of characteristics of a missional church, they would be in a position to establish strategies, vision and values statements, measurements, and goals for evaluating their churches in the light of these definitions. The next step would be to design programs to move these churches from where they currently are to this new description of what they should be like.

Luke does not address the crisis of Christian communities in this way. He takes a fundamentally different approach, paying careful attention to the actual questions and underlying narratives shaping the imagination of the people in these house churches. These are a people who feel the gospel story has somehow failed to match up to its promises. They've committed themselves to a way of life that promised a hopeful future, and now they find they are increasingly a harried minority living tenuous lives in an empire that is more and more suspicious of this new faith. What had happened?

Unfulfilled Hopes

Joel Green describes the social world in which Luke wrote as rampant with eschatological expectation.

> [E]schatological hope in its myriad forms focused preeminently on the coming of God to rule in peace and justice . . . that eschatological hope in the Lucan narrative must be read against a sociopolitical backdrop. This is true inasmuch as the coming of God would bring an end to political dominance and social oppression.[4]

Those to whom the gospel had come received it in the context of this eschatological hope. The resurrection and ascension of Jesus as the Christ signaled the coming of God's kingdom, the reign of God over the whole creation. This hope was now indissolubly tied to the promised return of Jesus who would bring to completion the kingdom of God. These expectations were part of the essential narrative of the gospel as it spread across the Roman world. The liberating Messiah, Jesus, would change the way the world was ruled.

This eschatological hope was rooted in the expectations of the Hebrew Scriptures. Recalling the words of the prophets, there was an expectation that Jesus would return to Jerusalem, and, specifically, to the temple from where he would initiate the peaceable kingdom of God. It would be from the temple that waters would flow out spreading to the four corners of the earth. Wherever these waters flowed, the earth would turn verdant with the lush produce of the earth. All the nations of the earth would be drawn toward Jerusalem and the temple where they would finally bend their knees and give their swords to the Lord and King of the whole creation.

These are the antecedents, in one form or another, of the eschatological expectation undergirding faithfulness to the gospel. The sociopolitical roots of the gospel in its spread across the empire cannot be set aside through some modern rereading of the texts in terms of a purely internal, personal, private salvation event. In the time of Luke's writing, the expectation was the consummation of God's reign in the coming of Jesus as Lord. This consummation would radically change and realign the sociopolitical and economic realities of the world. It is in this context that Mary's song in Luke 1:46–55 and Jesus's own Nazareth inaugural in Luke 4:16–30 are to be understood.

Crisis of Identity

Yet none of the promised events had taken place. It wasn't just that everything was delayed and more patience was required. Rather, by the latter part of the first century, the possibility of their coming to fruition seemed beyond hope. So much had taken place in these intervening years that this eschatological expectation, based on the promises in the narratives of Scripture for the reign of God, had been shredded in the realpolitik of Rome's mighty and cruel response to any group that refused to accept the totality of its narrative. The crisis these realities created could not be met simply by coming up with a fresh set of tactics, but called for a fundamental retheologizing of what God was about in the life, death, resurrection, and ascension of Jesus and the outpouring of the Spirit in the world.

It wasn't as if there were no story whatsoever to look back on. The stunning spread of the gospel from a small subsect of Judaism to a movement throughout the world could not be set aside. The ways in which the Good News of Jesus brought hope, transformation, and liberation to those cast aside on the garbage heap of the empire, and the ways in which these house church communities so often demonstrated and lived out the reality of a new social order that crossed ethnic and cultural divides could not be easily dismissed. The gospel of Jesus brought a new dynamic into the world, causing undeniable transformation in people. The radical nature of this gospel that Paul and others proclaimed as they spread across the empire was, indeed, good news for many. All of this was true. But it was wrapped in the context of the expectations outlined above. These narratives of transformation operated within a specific language house of eschatological hope. By the latter part of the first century, that hope seemed completely out of reach. These Gentile Christians faced a crisis of identity. What had gone wrong?

It would seem, on the face of it, that a lot had gone wrong. In Judea eschatological expectation over the reign of God reached such a pitch that in AD 70 a revolt broke out against Rome, with the full expectation that in this precipitant event God's armies would break in on the side of the rebellion, defeating Rome and establishing the kingdom of God on earth. The result of the long, protracted rebellion was utter devastation. Nero sent his armies, under the command of Vespasian, to crush the revolt with lethal Roman efficiency and vengeance. While resistance to Rome continued at Masada until around 74, the city of Jerusalem was quickly taken and its citizens put to the sword. As a city in revolt against the empire, it was razed to the ground. The temple was destroyed; the city and its environs were salted, symbolizing that nothing was to grow or flourish around it from that time forth. A new Jewish Diaspora was begun as Rome refused any Jew permission to live or be in the vicinity of Jerusalem. These events were a devastating blow to expectations of the kingdom of God.

By the late seventies these events, coupled with a spreading suspicion and Roman antagonism of the Christian communities within its empire, had created the crisis of identity described by Bosch. Without Jerusalem and the temple, what was to be made of the gospel story with its word of hope in the reign of God? Given that the basis for this eschatological hope had been destroyed, what was the meaning of Jesus's coming, and what was God up to in the world? Rome was supposed to bow its knee to this Lord and Christ, but now, it seemed, Rome had proved the superiority of its iron fist through the raw power of its armies.

Hard Realities

By the eighties, Emperor Domitian was reacting to revolts across the empire with increasing cruelty. He was solidifying Rome's power and authority by declaring himself, as emperor, to be the divine source of God's beneficence. Thus the reign of God and eschatological hope were confronted with a new, virulent Rome that would tolerate no counterclaims to its power, including a God who promised a different kingdom. It must have felt to these early Christians that something quite fundamental had gone wrong with the gospel and its message of hope to which they had so openly given themselves.

Added to these hard realities was the fact that even the Jewish people had rejected Jesus as God's Messiah, the fulfiller of the promises of Scripture. This fact, coupled with the sociopolitical realities summarized above, could only have deepened the confusion among Gentile Christians. Their consternation and confusion around the response of Jesus's own people were sources of much wrestling among the writers of the New Testament. John's prologue reflects this in the words: "He came to His own, and His own did not receive Him" (John 1:11 NKJV). Much of the book of Romans represents Paul's wrestling with the question of why Jesus's own people had rejected him as the Promised One of God. By the latter part of the first century, this separation between a diasporic Judaism and the nascent communities of Jesus across the empire was established. Indeed, in synagogues of the Diaspora, liturgies in one form or another were developed as a means of keeping any who professed Jesus as Lord from their midst. David Bosch summarizes the overall situation in this way:

The Christian church, which began as a renewal movement within Judaism, had, during the preceding four decades or so, undergone an almost complete transformation. . . . It had, in fact, for all intents and purposes become a Gentile church. . . . Yet the heyday of missionary expansion and of Paul's energetic outreach in all directions already lay a quarter century back and a degree of stagnation had set in. The church was now a church of the second generation and revealed all the characteristics of a movement that no longer shared the fervor and dedication of recent converts. The return of Christ, which was so fervently expected by the first generation of believers, did not take place. The faith of the church was tested in at least two ways: from within, there was a flagging of enthusiasm; from without, there was hostility and opposition from both Jews and pagans. In addition, Gentile Christians were facing a crisis of identity. They were asking: "Who are we really? How do we relate to the Jewish past. . . . Above all, how do we relate to the earthly Jesus, who is gradually and irrevocably receding into the past?"[5]

Important points of contact exist between the context of our discussion about the nature of the missional challenge being faced by the churches of North America and the crisis of identity among first-century Gentile Christians. Still shaped by a Eurocentric Reformation, Christians of North America address a deepening identity crisis by continuing to wrestle with fundamentally ecclesiocentric questions about how to make the church work in the midst of a cultural space of multiple narratives where the dominance of a settled, denominational, Eurocentric ecclesiology has less and less relevance.

Questions

In the context of this conversation, the questions being raised by the Gentile Christians to whom Luke was writing can be stated in the following terms:

1. What's gone wrong?
2. What is God up to in the world?
3. What, then, does it mean to be the church in this new space?

This is not to suggest Gentile Christians had compiled just this list of questions or that Luke was sitting down to write a two-volume response. They are, however, in the mix of the crisis that had to be addressed.

The proposal of this book is that these are precisely the questions that lie just under the surface for a North American church still lost in a monologue about its own health, effectiveness, style, growth, and future. The following chapters look at the ways Luke responded to these questions as a means of framing what a missional engagement of the gospel with our culture(s) might involve.

8

The Boundary-Breaking Spirit

Seeing Luke-Acts through a Language House Lens

One can imagine how easy it would have been for first-century Christians to wonder what had gone wrong. The language house within which these Gentile Christians had lived was one shaped by a particular set of expectations around the ways their eschatological hope was to be fulfilled (the imminent return of Christ and the overcoming of Rome as it bowed the knee to this new Lord of all creation). With these expectations dashed, it was clear that the language house within which they had lived was not sustainable in this new reality. What were the alternatives? How does a social group go about discovering, constructing, and living in a different language house?

Luke turns his attention to these questions because he understands that until these small communities can discover a different narrative, a different way of understanding what God was about in Jesus, they would be stuck in these other narratives and, therefore, unable to enter the new space of Christian life that had emerged by the end of the first century. Luke's approach to addressing this crisis was to retheologize the events of the past fifty-odd years. He would tell the story of Jesus and the birth of the church from Jerusalem onward to provide these Gentiles with a different language house for seeing what God was doing in the world and how to be a faithful people in this new space.

This and the following chapters will sketch out how Luke went about this work of retheologizing and will frame the ways in which the churches of North America might also respond to the new space where so many of them now find themselves. These chapters are not meant as a commentary on Luke-Acts but as a reading of some ways in which this creative theologian sought to reorient communities back to the ways of God in the world.

Jesus, Judaism, and Eschatological Hope

The way we tell stories says a lot about the language houses in which we live. In two distinct events early in Acts, the young church is challenged to explain what is happening in Jerusalem as, literally, thousands of people on pilgrimage from all over the Diaspora are drawn into this new movement of Judaism that sees Jesus as the Lord who fulfills Scripture.[1] The first event is at Pentecost when the Spirit comes on the crowds gathered in the city for festival in such a way that each is hearing, in his own language, the words of the apostles.

Peter is compelled to respond to the social imaginary of the cultured Greek Diaspora Jews, whose immediate response was to label the disciples as ignorant, babbling Galileans. Peter's address in Acts 2 is not just a defense of the disciples' sobriety but an argument for the gospel, constructed from within the narrative expectations of the Jewish Scriptures. His response is filled with direct quotes from and allusions to the promises of what God would do "in those days," an allusion to the eschatological hope of Israel.

Peter addressed the hope and expectation of the Diaspora in terms of the kingdom of God, locating that expectation in the life, death, and resurrection of Jesus and the resultant pouring out of the Spirit as the sign of "those last days." The point here, however, is that Peter's interpretation and framing of events is all done *within* the language house of Israel and Judaism. Nothing in his presentation suggests a bigger picture. When, for example, he quotes from the prophet Joel: "In the last days . . . I will pour out my Spirit on all people" (Acts 2:17), this is not a reference to the universal movement of God in and for the whole world. It is an argument for why seemingly ignorant Galileans could be expressing the purposes and actions of God in such a way that all those from the language worlds of the Diaspora could understand.

How to account for this is straightforward for Peter. In the new era of the Spirit, promised with the coming of God's Promised One, this is precisely what is to be expected. The new era brought about in Jesus and through the outpouring of the Spirit results in an egalitarian community that no longer discriminates between man and woman, servant and free. The coming of the Spirit in Jerusalem, declares Peter, has created this radically new situation.

In his announcement, however, it appears that for Peter, and the disciples as a whole, the community of Jesus in Jerusalem expresses the fulfillment of Israel's hope for God's reign. It is the fulfillment of God's promises within a Jerusalem-centered (Jewish) movement. There is no hint of a radically different imagination that would involve the whole world. This observation is intended not as a criticism but as a description of the language house shaping the church from its beginning. There may not have been another way for those disciples to frame the meaning of Pentecost—but the point is that, at the start, Pentecost was interpreted within a specific set of ethnic, national assumptions.

This focus is further evidenced in Stephen's speech to the Sanhedrin, which placed Jesus's life, death, and resurrection at the center of Israel's eschatological hopes and showed how the hardness of previous generations and the present leadership blinded them to what God was doing for Israel. Again, given the context and the situation, the focus of Stephen's apologetic is to be expected. What is absent from his speech, however (and bear in mind Luke is writing to Gentiles struggling with questions of what has gone wrong), is any reference to the meaning of the gospel for those outside the house of Israel.

The community of Jesus, founded at Pentecost, is one that frames itself as the fulfillment of Israel's hopes. In this sense its self-understanding was within the context of Judaism. It did not have the global perspective that would emerge out of hard, bitter conflict. Just as many North American churches still assume the Reformation, in terms of its theologies and ecclesial formations, to be normative and the primary interpretive grid for the Christian narrative, so this young church assumed its Judaism was the interpretive grid for all that God had set loose in Jesus and the Spirit.

Parallels to the Reformation

The parallel between the early church and the church following the Reformation is instructive. African missiologist Jehu Hanciles, who now lives in North America, in describing the sixteenth-century Euro-tribal movements that came to be known under the generic title Reformation, states:

> The sixteenth century Protestant reformations shattered the structural uniformity of medieval Catholicism . . . and paved the way for national Christian identities. But the Protestant reformations left the underlying construct of Christendom intact. . . . The Protestant movement may be regarded as the *"renewal of Christendom."* . . . Europe would henceforth, to all intents and purposes, be a continent characterized by two dominant forms of faith, each adopted as the official religion within the territorial limits of particular nation-states. Protestantism was now "confined chiefly to the Teutonic peoples," or

peoples of Germanic origin . . . and it was mainly through the efforts of these people that the Protestant forms of Christianity would be "propagated by *migration* and conversion."[2]

It was in this sense that the Protestant mission was the *westernization* of other peoples, from the perspective of a deeply ethnocentric outlook, as if to become a follower of Jesus required becoming in a whole series of ways an adherent and convert to Western ways of life. In a similar way this was the movement of the young communities of Jesus birthed and gathered in Jerusalem. The movement of Jesus was the fulfillment of an ethnocentric, tribal religion. Movement into the community of Jesus was a movement into, a grafting into, this ethnic tribe.

Luke's Invitation

Luke writes his narrative about the birth and development of the church with the background of Gentile communities in the late seventies, who will be reading these texts, in view. They know that everything has changed since Pentecost. How was Luke crafting these stories to answer the questions of what had gone wrong and what, therefore, God was doing in the world? In brief, Luke addresses these questions with a single response: nothing has gone wrong! He does this not out of some naive optimism or because he is shaped by the power of positive thinking but because he dwells in a different language house from his Gentile readers. Luke grasps the crisis of identity confronting these Gentile Christians but understands it as a failure of imagination; the narrative framework into which they have put the stories of Jesus and the expectations of God's reign were too confining, too narrow in their scope.

His intention is to retell the founding stories of the young church in order to construct a radically different language house for his readers. In Luke-Acts he is inviting these little communities in the midst of the empire into a different imagination. Luke's basic approach is to write the story of everything that Jesus began to do and teach to show that, right from the beginning in Jerusalem, God was up to something much bigger than the little boxes into which these initiating communities had placed him. The way of expressing this is through an accounting of the acts of the Holy Spirit. One of the purposes in this way of writing the story is to suggest, by implication, that these second-generation Gentile Christians were, likewise, putting the movement of God in too small a box and, thereby, missing what God was accomplishing in the world.

Persecution and Dispersion

"Nothing has gone wrong" is a bold statement in light of the previous thirty-odd years and the eschatological hope that had seemed so central to the missionary spread of the gospel across the empire. Yet this is precisely what Luke is saying. How was Luke interpreting those generative years? Several events in the early chapters of Acts help us see the ways Luke frames this part of his response to the question of what had gone wrong.

First, there are a series of events that cluster around the stoning of Stephen. Emboldened by this killing, a broader persecution breaks out against the community of Jesus in Jerusalem and spreads into surrounding cities. This is a period that must have come shortly after Pentecost, when Saul, threatening the slaughter of believers, asked permission to go to the synagogues in Damascus and root out any who were of the Way and bring them bound to Jerusalem and prison (Acts 9:1–2). This reference to Damascus so early on suggests how quickly the Way was dispersing and moving out into the broader Jewish communities away from Jerusalem. Damascus was a full week's walk—no small distance for the period—but already there were synagogues that must have been shaped by a new belief in Jesus as the One who fulfills the promises of Scripture, just as Peter and Stephen had said.

Then the concern of official Jewish leadership must have been about the fact that Jerusalem had been filled with Diaspora Jews who were returning to their home cities and towns across the empire carrying with them the virus of this new movement. This would have resulted in high anxiety, as exhibited by Saul's zeal. One can sense the urgency. Like national health organizations around the world in 2009 trying desperately to control H1N1, the Jewish leadership sought to stamp out this virus as quickly as possible. Saul's request to the Sanhedrin indicates what was going on—these people of the Way were going to synagogues in other towns and cities telling Jews in the regions about Jerusalem and beyond that Jesus was the One who had come to fulfill the eschatological hopes of Israel.

The movement of Jesus was spreading quickly out from Jerusalem through to Judea and Samaria and, most important, it was understood and practiced as a movement within Judaism. There's no indication or mention of movement across the boundaries of Judaism to Gentile believers. Luke uses Acts 9–13 as a pivotal shift in this dynamic to show that the language house of the disciples at this point wasn't sufficient to contain what the Spirit was doing. Acts 9 reports that there's a period of peace when the young church seems to have a good reputation with Judaism and is growing. At the same time there are also reports of persecution in Jerusalem that forces many of the Christians out of the city toward the coastal regions. These stories of persecution seem to be told in the midst of a new tension around the place of Gentiles in the movement of Jesus.

In Acts 11:19 we are told Christians have been scattered out of Jerusalem because of the stoning of Stephen. This must have been connected with the persecution that involved Saul and Damascus. Luke picks up this thread of the story even though it probably happened some time earlier. In the meantime Peter, for example, had the freedom to go to places like Lydda, Joppa, and then Caesarea to heal the sick and teach about the Way. What is important about the scattering from Jerusalem is the description of what these Jewish Christians did and by implication didn't do. They traveled out as far as Phoenicia, Cyprus, and Antioch but "they spoke the word to no one except Jews" (v. 19 NRSV). It's hard to escape the circumscribed context within which the movement of Jesus was expected to operate. Even in the movement out from Jerusalem, this understanding of Jesus as fulfillment *within Judaism* directed the actions of the church.

Boundary Breaking

Within this context, Acts 9–11 takes on new meaning. Peter travels northwest from Jerusalem to Lydda, a Jewish town, where he heals a Hellenistic Jew. Then he goes to Joppa where there is further healing. With Peter in Joppa, the context is correct for his dream about the clean and unclean food. Three times in the dream, God invites Peter to eat the food being offered. Each time Peter's response is the same: "By no means, Lord; for I have never eaten anything that is profane or unclean" (10:15 NRSV). The dream is the prelude to Peter's meeting with Cornelius. It establishes the clear, inviolable boundary within which Peter's (and hence, the whole church's) language house had been set. There is a clear, nonnegotiable boundary to following God and, by implication, there is a clear, nonnegotiable boundary around what it means to be a follower of Jesus. Peter knew that, just as you don't eat anything unclean, so you don't go around speaking the word about Jesus to those who are not Jews.

This is the point Luke is making. The imagination and language house of the Jerusalem-formed church were bound within these lines of meaning. Luke is making it clear that these are the ways in which the young church is forming and circumscribing its life. It is against this background that Luke shapes an alternative narrative, addressing the question of what's gone wrong.

Not according to Jewish Law

The action of Acts 11 is written in sparse, tight, fast-paced narrative. A lot is happening that is disrupting the expectations and settled rhythms that seemed to be characterizing the early Jerusalem community. Opposition and persecution from the Jewish leadership in Jerusalem are becoming more intense and focused. At the same time the tight boundaries of the Jesus movement are pushed apart by fresh developments that are really outside the control and planning of the church's leaders, like Peter and James. Herod has a hand in the opposition (chap. 12). James, the brother of Jesus, is killed. Peter is seized and thrown in jail. The ground is shifting quickly. Alongside these events that are related to Jewish leaders are other, even more disquieting happenings.

To understand Acts 11:20, we must first look at the events that shape Peter's encounters a little earlier in verses 12–18. Immediately after Peter's trance in Joppa, he is brought to Caesarea to meet with a Roman (read "Gentile") centurion named Cornelius. It is too facile to describe these events as some natural, linear movement of the church from one stage to another. This would miss the dynamics of Luke's developing response to the question of what had gone wrong. As part of Luke's answer, we see Peter brought face-to-face with a Gentile. Cornelius is described as a "God-fearer," which might be read as an indication of a developmental, progressive movement of the gospel as it now connects with Gentiles who were considering conversion to Judaism. In Luke's hands, however, this event is a radical break that involves Peter but over which Peter has no control.

Luke writes that, even as Peter struggles to speak to Cornelius, "the Holy Spirit fell upon them just as it had upon us at the beginning" (v. 15 NRSV). Luke is establishing that this conversion of a Gentile to the Way of Jesus was not as a result of Peter's decision (he is wrestling with what to do even standing before Cornelius). The narrative unfolds in a way that suggests it is the

Spirit who makes the event happen and so crosses the boundaries of Jewish law.

Beyond Neat Categories

It is in this context that we are invited to read those other events in Acts 11:19–22 where these Jewish Christians (likely of both Jerusalem and the Diaspora), who had been speaking the Word only to other Jews, suddenly cross a huge boundary. Being led by the Spirit, they jump the Jewish/God-fearer barrier, and "a great number became believers and turned to the Lord" (v. 21 NRSV).

We know that significant conflict broke out over the admission of Gentiles into the community of Jesus. The leaders in Jerusalem sent Barnabas to assess the situation because events seemed to be moving beyond their control. What had happened in Joppa and now in far greater numbers in Antioch didn't fit their language house and threatened to undermine some of their most basic assumptions about the nature of this Jesus movement. All of this would lead to ruptures both in relationships and, eventually, between Judaism and the church.

Long after these events had happened, Luke was weaving together the stories of conflict and rupture to create a new language house for Gentile Christians. He was providing an interpretive framework to address the larger question of what had gone wrong.

At a fundamental level, nothing had gone wrong. From the beginning, the young church had located the movement of Jesus entirely within the language house of Judaism as its fulfillment. The eschatological expectations were shaped around this narrative. It is clear from the way Luke tells these stories that the movement's leaders, people like James and Peter, saw themselves shaping a Jewish movement that would graft in some Hellenizing God-fearers. But in these passages something else is going on. The Spirit of God comes to break the boundaries. The boundary-breaking work was not a normal, natural development nor was it the result of any leader; it was the Spirit breaking into the settled assumptions and established rhythms in a way that reframes the meaning of Jesus's life, death, and resurrection.

The subtext present here is that God is doing something through Jesus that is much bigger than all the small, neat categories and boxes in which the movement of God had been placed, boxes such as Jerusalem, temple, synagogue, and Jewish followers of the fulfilled Messiah. These language houses had to be shaken and taken apart. So the Spirit came to break the boundaries. Nothing had gone wrong except that the Spirit of God would not allow this sedimentation of meaning nor the practices that follow.

This boundary-breaking work of the Spirit creates conflict, consternation, and confusion. It leaves people struggling to figure out how the things they thought normative to the gospel fit into this shifting of boundaries, which at one time seemed so clear and well-defined. The reason for this boundary-breaking work of the Spirit is that God is about something in the world that is far bigger than the confines of an ethnotribal religion even if that ethnotribal religion is the Judaism of the Scriptures. There is a cosmic scope to this gospel, and the Spirit will not leave the church forever sitting inside its well-defined boxes that try to determine what God can do in the world.[3] Hence, in these early days the boundaries are crossed, the assumptions are broken, and the church is set on a whole new journey as the agents of God's future.

Implications for the North American Church

Luke has given a theological reading of what happened to the post-ascension movement of the church. He provides a theological reading on the events that would tear apart the boundaries of God's people. In so doing he is inviting these late-first-century Gentile Christians into a different language house with the narrative understanding that the Spirit of God will continue to come and break the boundaries of our small, narrow, confined assumptions about what God is up to in the world. God is out there ahead continuing the work of bringing all things together in Jesus Christ.

This retheologizing of the events of the young church has important implications for the life of the North American church in our time. Across denominations and long-established church organizations is a deepening anxiety about what it means to be God's people in our day. For many in church leadership in the West, the question lurks just beneath the surface: what's gone wrong?

What if the answer to this question is similar to the one Luke gave in Acts? What if the life-giving Spirit is saying to us that nothing has gone wrong but that he is breaking apart the five-hundred-year-old boxes in which we have so conveniently placed the movement of God since the European Protestant reformations? What if the period we are in is another one of those times when the boundary-breaking Spirit is pushing apart the settled, managed, and controlled ecclesiologies that came out of a specific period of European history with its nation-states and the emergence of its hegemony over the world? What if the great shifts of global populations, which have changed the face of continents, are all elements of this boundary-breaking work of the Spirit in our time? In the midst of these shifting worlds, what if the ending of the ecclesiological monologue is another part of this boundary-breaking work? Nothing has gone wrong! The God of Jesus Christ is still shaping the new creation. What then do we do when the Spirit breaks the boundaries?

9

The Strange New Ways of God

Sending the Seventy—a Guide for Our Times

In Acts and then in his Gospel, Luke is writing a narrative about God's actions in the world to fulfill eschatological hopes that had energized Israel and, then, the young church. He is shaping an account of God's redemptive purposes for the entire world in a way that shows the faithfulness of God. This is intended to invite Gentile communities facing a crisis of identity to trust the actions of God in the face of what appears to be a failure of expectation. Luke will show that the issue is not God's faithfulness but the narrow ways in which the gospel had been understood. In Acts he does this by emphasizing the boundary-breaking actions of the Spirit in the midst of resistance and conflict from religious and civil authorities as well as from within the young community.

The backdrop within which Luke writes, therefore, is one of conflict. From the birth accounts to Jesus's struggles with the Jewish leadership to his arrest and crucifixion, this motif of struggle and conflict shapes Luke's work. The young community fares no better.

Too quickly it is propelled into similar conflicts that run through Acts; in the final chapters the outcome is far from clear and nothing is wrapped up and tied with a neat bow.

In both Luke and Acts the conflict continues and the ambiguity about the outcome is not removed, but through it all Luke's story line shows that God is at work shaping a whole new world. Some of the conflicts internal to the young community in Acts were born of expectations and assumptions of how and where God was going to work, especially the taken-for-granted conviction that the Jesus movement, as a completion of Judaism, was an essentially Jewish movement. In describing the work of the Holy Spirit as the boundary-breaking presence of God who will not permit these Christians to define, settle, and manage the little boxes into which they placed the movement of Jesus, Luke is inviting his Gentile audience to embrace an alternative narrative and language house to the one they had been given in terms of eschatological hopes.

I want to suggest this same pattern of events is at work among North American Christians today, and the Spirit has continued to be boundary-breaking. The churches formed from the Euro-tribal religious reformations of the sixteenth century established forms of ecclesial practice and theologies that have been assumed determinative not just for European–North American cultures in a specific time but for all cultures in all times and places.

This sense that the important questions about the church and its relationships with the cultures have been addressed in the reformations of that period created a situation, described in part one, that assumed the primacy of ecclesiology to the point that all else (gospel and cultures, for example) are about the development of tactics to adjust and engage changing circumstances. This is the language house in which churches continue to live.

Part two has been looking at Luke-Acts as a means of assessing how we might find fresh ways to understand our own situation. We can understand our own time as one in which the Spirit of God is breaking the boundaries within which the Christian movement has operated in the Western context. Not only is this boundary-breaking about a reductionistic preoccupation with the church as the central idea we have to get right (the so-called "essence" of the church issue), but it is also about the tradition of theologizing that came out of the sixteenth-century reformations in Europe. In a rapidly globalizing West, now characterized by new and massive people movements from many other parts of the world, this "Reformation" boundary may also be one the Spirit is breaking.

In Acts, Luke is reorienting the hope and expectation of Gentile believers. In the midst of confusion and a crisis of identity, it is possible to read the circumstances in a very different manner. The established language house for understanding eschatological hope in terms of Jerusalem, temple, Jewishness, and the empire's embrace was too small a box in which to place the radical announcement of good news in Jesus and the birth of the Jesus community. The good news is that God is doing something far bigger and more imaginative than can be placed in these small, parochial categories. The crisis of identity is not a crisis concerning God's purposes but comes as a result of the narrow ways in which early Christians experienced and structured God's purposes after Pentecost. Luke is inviting his Gentile readers into a different language house. While it opens up a new space for hope and a radically new context for theologizing and practicing the gospel in towns and villages, it also raised a whole new set of questions.

Raising New Questions

Within the old language house of expectation, certain questions could be easily answered in terms of the Jerusalem/temple/empire narratives. But in this different economy of God's actions that the Spirit has burst open for the first-century Christians, how does one know what God is doing in the world? How does one decide what it means to be the church in this new language house—where the old explanations of how things work no longer cohere? These were questions that needed answers if the Gentile churches were to address their crisis of identity. They are also the questions we have to answer in our day.

If it is the case that God's Spirit is breaking the boundaries of ecclesial life in the Western churches because they can no longer contain the ways in which the Spirit is at work in the world, then these nonecclesiocentric questions of what God is doing must be addressed. If the ecclesiocentricity of our conversations is now, in fact, a barrier and boundary the Spirit is in the process of breaking apart, then it is urgent that we answer these other questions.

The boundary-breaking Spirit is making it clear to a growing number of people that ecclesiocentricity has little future. The hope in this difficult discovery is that there are also new, strange questions we haven't needed to think about before. When the church lay at the center of the conversation, it was relatively simple to name what God was up to, and we had endless books that defined and described what it meant to be the church. In this new space, where the church is not the central focus or question, how do we go about addressing these new questions? How will we know what God is doing when the answers can't be taken for granted? How do we know what it means to be the church when the church is no longer the central preoccupation?

The rest of this chapter proposes that we can discover answers to these questions in Luke's Gospel. Rather than engage the whole Gospel, this chapter will focus on Luke 10:1–12. The proposal is that in this text we can discern a way in which Luke continued to frame a response to Gentile Christians faced with their own crisis of identity, and it can, therefore, offer us a way of understanding how to be faithful to the gospel in our time.

A Proposal for Reading Our Time of Crisis

As I have said, the Spirit breaks boundaries, a work that can be for us disorienting and disturbing. The well-worn patterns of Christian life that shaped the once dominant European-immigrant churches are eroding as our whole world enters a new and as yet undefined space.[1] The patterns of Christian life that shaped and gave meaning to Christian life in North America for much of the twentieth century, especially convictions about the place of the church, are breaking apart. How do we figure out what God is doing in the world? It is only as we focus attention on this primary question that we can ever ask what it means to be the church in this new space—but this is a secondary question at this point.

Luke may not have had just these questions in mind when he wrote his Gospel. He did, however, write with an eye toward Gentile communities in crisis that needed help in reorienting their imaginations. The following sections of this chapter imagine what Luke's response would have been to these questions as he tells the story of the sending of the seventy to all the places Jesus intended to go as he set his eyes toward Jerusalem and his suffering. Luke's readers already knew the outcome of this journey with its rising opposition toward Jesus and then the post-Pentecost communities. What I propose is that in retelling this story, Luke is retheologizing for these Gentiles the question of what God is doing in the world and, therefore, how to be the church.

The proposal offered in the following sections is that Luke 10:1–12 describes a way of breaking the church monologue and opening up to us a radically different way of being God's people. It is an example of what Lesslie Newbigin meant about becoming cross-cultural missionaries in our own culture. Such a missionary steps out of the monologue. He or she isn't preoccupied with self. When entering a different culture, this missionary knows that he or she can't begin the conversation with church questions. Even as a young missionary in India, Newbigin, who had gone with all the educational training and culture of British university life, realized he would be of no good to the kingdom unless he learned to enter the culture and dwell among the people to whom he had come. He made a practice of living with and sitting among the people in the towns and villages to which he had been sent. This sitting in their midst was one of the ways he sought to be present to them and attend to their stories, for he knew that until he did this, he would not be able to understand the gospel in this new place. In the midst of these listening dialogues, he learned to be present to the other, to hear, read, and *perform* the gospel in ways he couldn't have imagined.

Dwell in the Story

Luke 10:1–12 speaks into our crisis in a similar way. The text is presented below—it's important to read the Scripture, because we might assume we already know it. When working with communities of Christians, I invite them to read this text as often as possible, over and over again, until it starts to live inside them. Dwell in this story, seeking to hear what the Spirit might be saying to us through the text.

> After this the Lord appointed seventy-two others and sent them two by two ahead of him to every town and place where he was about to go. He told them, "The harvest is plentiful, but the workers are few. Ask the Lord of the harvest, therefore, to send out workers into his harvest field. Go! I am sending you out like lambs among wolves. Do not take a purse or bag or sandals; and do not greet anyone on the road.
>
> "When you enter a house, first say, 'Peace to this house.' If a man of peace is there, your peace will rest on him; if not, it will return to you. Stay in that house, eating and drinking whatever they give you, for the worker deserves his wages. Do not move around from house to house.
>
> "When you enter a town and are welcomed, eat what is set before you. Heal the sick who are there and tell them, 'The kingdom of God is near you.' But when you enter a town and are not welcomed, go into its streets and say, 'Even the dust of your town that sticks to our feet we wipe off against you. Yet be sure of this: The kingdom

of God is near.' I tell you, it will be more bearable on that day for Sodom than for that town."

The ways this text shapes our responses to the questions of what God is up to in the world and what it means to be the church surprise us. This narrative asks us to turn away from deep patterns of response.

Radical Discipleship

The narrative begins in the context of discipleship. In other portions of Scripture, we read of numbers of people coming up to Jesus and asking what they need to do to become disciples. His responses were so counterintuitive to their expectations and desires that they turned away from Jesus. (For example, he tells a rich, young ruler to go and sell all he has and then come back and follow him.) This discipleship is more radical than anything anyone has imagined. It is not about fixing something or adjusting small areas of one's life. This discipleship requires a very different kind of response and it will probably not align with our expectations or fit with the categories of meaning that have shaped us to this point in our lives.

It is after these encounters with would-be disciples that Jesus sends out seventy followers ahead of him to all the towns and villages where he intends to go in Galilee of the Gentiles.[2]

This story is set in the midst of Jesus's journey down to Jerusalem where he will lose his life. Almost the entire Gospel from this point forward is built around the journey south, its results, and the resurrection. While we now know the story well, for those listening to its first readings, it was filled with huge surprises and turns that no one could have imagined. The events that were foreseen in the story were unexpected; nothing seemed to fit the established norms.

For Luke this had to do with the why and way these seventy are sent out. For the second-generation Gentile Christians spread across the empire who were reading the Gospel, what must it have meant for them, as they were reading about their Lord's journey to Jerusalem and death, to come on this story? What would it have been saying to their questions about the crisis of identity and meaning they faced?

In Luke 9:51–56 Jesus and the disciples encounter opposition from a Samaritan village. They were not welcomed because "he was heading for Jerusalem." Old animosities flare up. The disciples respond with the same old formula from a language house that viscerally reacts to Samaritans: "Call down fire on the village and blot out these no good Samaritans! Teach a lesson of power and authority; show them who's in charge once and for all." Jesus will have none of it; he will not get embroiled in the fight despite hard opposition and no recognition of who he is.

Luke is helping his readers understand that opposition is the norm when the Spirit breaks the boundaries of expectations and predictable ways of relating to people. At each turn of this story, Luke is providing these second-generation Gentile Christians a radically different language house from which to reframe their imagination about the promises of God and their place in the movement of Jesus.

Following this encounter with the Samaritan town, a foretaste of Jerusalem—it's not just Samaritans who don't get it and resist—Jesus talks to the disciples about the cost of discipleship (vv. 57–62). There are going to be lots of people who want to follow the Jesus movement as long as it fits in with their settled assumptions of how things should turn out. But when the directions Jesus takes diverge from the expectations of what God is doing in the world, resistance is prompt and fierce. Luke does not pull his punches in orienting these Christians as they look back over half a century of the church's young life and wonder why it's no longer working the way it did for the first generations. This is the context in which he sets the story of the sending of the seventy.

At the conclusion of this story, immediately following their return from the towns and villages, Luke tells a very different story about Samaritans. This story, that of the good Samaritan, asks questions about welcoming the stranger and who is my neighbor. Luke is pointing to and anticipating that, apropos to the experience of the seventy, the Spirit is working even among the Gentiles; it means we have to be open to the strange new ways of God as boundaries are broken and expectations have to be reoriented.

Luke writes these stories of the sending of the seventy and the Samaritan on the road to suggest that what God is doing in the world has a lot more to do with being the stranger and receiving hospitality than being in control of the resources and the answers. Here expectations are turned upside down as it turns out that the strangers who need to be welcomed are those being sent. What could this mean for those of us asking disorienting questions about what God is up to in the world and what it means to be the church? We need to unwrap the story further.

Leaving Baggage Behind

A number of elements need to be explored for us to understand what is probably happening in this passage. In the first place, the number of disciples Jesus sends gives us clues about Luke's intention. In Jewish tradition it is seventy elders who are commissioned to translate the law from Hebrew to Greek; in Luke's hands this is an allusion to the mission of God to the whole world. In other Jewish texts, such as Genesis 10, the number of nations in the world is seventy. So the context of the sending is the anticipated mission of the gospel to the whole world (in the book of Acts).

Jesus's instructions to his disciples strike readers as peculiar. He says, "Go! I am sending you out like lambs among wolves. Do not take a purse or bag or sandals; and do not greet anyone on the road" (Luke 10:3–4). They were not to take a lot of baggage with them on their journey. In essence they were not to depend on their own resources. In the context of the first century, these followers were sent out on their mission as *strangers* who would be in need of hospitality from people of the towns and villages. Luke is suggesting that the mission of God moves forward in the world when disciples of Jesus choose to become like strangers in the towns and villages *so they will be dependent on the hosts.*

The story of this sending, therefore, is not only to illustrate the mission of God to the whole world but also to show the manner in which this mission is to be carried out. It is radically different from the conceptions of mission that characterize the Euro-Protestant churches of our time. In the ancient Middle East, strangers were an important part of the overall cultural matrix. They were the outsiders who, for one reason or another, were dependent on the hospitality of others for their survival, and there were strict laws about how the stranger was to be treated.

But this was a two-way street. In such a culture, the village people took in the stranger because they knew that at any time in the future they or their children might become strangers themselves and need to be taken in. There was a deep mutuality in this relationship to the stranger. It is important to understand what lies behind the allusion here if we are to have an idea of God's intention. It appears there is a connection, a link between being in the place of the stranger in need and being able to discern God's working in the world. The story is suggesting that the one is a precursor of the other.

In the Old Testament story of Elijah, this dynamic is at work (see 1 Kings 17). After Ahab and his Baalist wife, Jezebel, kill the prophets of Israel, Elijah flees to the Kerith ravine where he is fed for a time by ravens (note the connections that we will need to pick up later—being in the place of a stranger in need and finding the place where food is given—these are also connected in Luke's story). Elijah must move on because there is no water in that part of the desert—he is genuinely a man outside his own context and in need of help from someone. The Lord directs him to the city of Zarephath (a Gentile city of Baal worshipers—Jezebel's own people), where he meets a widow who provides hospitality to this Jew (see also Luke

4:25–26 where Jesus references the widow of Zarephath and Elijah in response to opposition in Nazareth). Elijah, with nothing, dwells in the house of the widow and, in that context, discovers again what God is calling him to do. Elijah must dwell with the other to discern God's purposes. It meant that this Gentile woman could not be construed as the "enemy," the outsider who has nothing to give, but as the one who will provide the table around which Elijah might reimagine his vocation. It is boundary breaking.

This is the way in which Luke frames Jesus's sending of the seventy. The fascinating characteristic of Elijah's story is that he finds himself pushed outside his own community. He becomes a stranger because the world in which he functioned as a prophet of Israel has been taken from him. In this new and precarious space, Elijah is compelled to ask difficult questions about God and about the relationship between God and Israel.

This was also the situation of the Gentile Christians to whom Luke was writing. The parallel can be made in this way. Elijah's world was fundamentally disoriented when the assumptions he had about what God was doing were undermined. This also happened to these Gentile communities to whom Luke was writing. Elijah found answers to these questions of disorientation as he was forced outside his established world and placed in situations where he became dependent on the hospitality of those who should have been in need of his ministry. Is it the case that the boundary-breaking Spirit is placing these Gentile Christians in similar contexts? By extension, in our own time, will Christian communities in North America discover answers to their crisis of identity as they become willing to enter a similar experience of becoming like strangers who, without baggage, must enter the towns and villages to receive hospitality from the other?

Leaving baggage behind is a key part of what Luke is saying. This leaving baggage behind is about a radical reorientation of how to answer the question of what God is doing in our world. This is alien to and far away from the ways in which most churches "send" people into the towns and villages in which we live. Take evangelism programs as an example. Church evangelism or planting schemes call for very different ways of engaging people in neighborhoods and communities from what Luke is describing. Usually these programs set up some kind of category or measurement into which the people of a community are placed, including how close or distant they are from knowing Jesus on a scale of understanding or readiness for the gospel, how many contacts someone may have already had with a church prior to this encounter, and where a person is on a scale of openness or resistance to Christ. These plans seek to answer certain questions: What particular "seeker" type of program does the church have that outsiders would be interested in joining or attending? What needs do people have that a church program or Saturday night service might address? And so forth. In all these cases, the church sends people into the neighborhood fully armed with marketing research, methods of assessing the readiness of someone for a next step, and programs to offer. In other words, churches send out people with plenty of prepacked baggage.

We go into towns and villages with a huge amount of baggage. All of this baggage will continually blind us to what God is doing in the towns and villages where we live, because when we take the baggage, we assume we already know who the people are and what they need. All the questions of what God might be doing are already answered, catalogued, and turned into sellable programs and strategies.

When we send people out with baggage, we lose two things—the ability to see people and their needs as they really are and an openness to what God is doing. We objectify people. They are not the other who, like Newbigin, we must dwell among and be present to, but they are a category, for which we have plans. When this is our focus, we can't listen to the person who stands before us as a human being—he or she is the object of our plans. That's baggage of the worst kind.

In the second place, we have already determined what God is up to and, therefore, what needs to happen. But in the boundary-breaking work of the Spirit, this is precisely where we need a different approach. We cannot ask the questions of what God is up to in our neighborhoods and communities when we think we already know. It seems that Luke is trying to tell us something of critical importance in these brief instructions. In a time of boundary breaking, when settled assumptions of how God ought to work and what the church is supposed to be are undermined, when our assumptions about how it was all supposed to turn out are no longer viable, then we must take a radically different road. We must leave our baggage behind and be willing to become like a stranger in need of the welcome and care of the other if we stand any chance of answering the question, What is God up to in our world today?

Most of us are trying to figure out all the best, seeker-friendly ways to get someone to *come* to something we are offering. Our plans and what we want to achieve are all-important—another huge piece of baggage, which prevents our listening to and receiving from the other. Luke points in a different direction. This is a text that helps us sketch a new map of the road ahead. The language house of Eurocentric churches cannot provide the dominant story for being God's people in a post-Christendom, globalizing world.

"Journeying Sentness"

For Luke the faithful God sends the boundary-breaking Spirit to form communities of Jesus characterized by *journeying sentness*. This means that Luke, in writing his two volumes, used the mission of God in the world as one of the primary lenses for interpreting events to these Gentile communities. In one sense this is part of the question with which these Christians were wrestling, namely, What had gone wrong with the mission of God? Telling about the sending of the seventy is part of Luke's vigorous counternarrative, which says that the mission is still central but not in the ways anticipated.

The overall sense of this story is that Jesus sends his followers out on a counterintuitive journey of mission for the sake of the kingdom. This was probably a difficult metaphor for these second-generation Gentile Christians. Eschatological expectations had faltered. The heroes of the church's birthing, leaders like Paul and Peter who drove the mission of the kingdom across the Roman world, were gone from the stage, creating anxiety about who was leading and what the next steps might involve. Most would have grown up in house churches linked together by the stories of an expanding movement in which they had seen lots of people coming into the faith. Toward the end of the first century, as David Bosch points out, the situation was changing. These Christians probably didn't share the fervor of the earlier generation, so they were characterized by a loss of energy and enthusiasm for the mission of God. In the light of these realities, Bosch sees Luke returning to the founding stories of Jesus and the disciples to provide these Christians with a new basis for being faithful communities of witness.[3] And this would mean reshaping their imagination about how the Spirit was moving this witness of Jesus forward.

The metaphor of journeying faithfulness in the midst of opposition must have been a struggle for them to hear. By this juncture they may well have expected Jesus to return. By now God's future should have been wrapped up rather than this situation of crisis, conflict, and confusion. They were most likely communities that had been waiting, expecting; they had a predetermined conviction that there was but a short period before the eschatological future dawned. What would these changes in expectation mean for their formation as communities of witness? How could they go about discerning what God was doing? Luke's metaphors of discipleship and conflict, of journeying and entering communities without baggage, painted a wildly different interpretive framework from the one into which they had settled. The implication is that in the context of crisis and identity, it is a journeying people who are ready to risk entering the ambiguous and vulnerable spaces of mission that follow the contours of God's engagements in the world.

Ordinary People

By the latter part of the first century, the heroes of that initial outburst of missionary fervor were gone. What happens when the heroes, the great figures of the faith who pioneered an immense movement of the Spirit, are gone from the stage? Where do you turn to find new heroes who can lead into the crisis-ridden future? Luke's answer is different from anything that could have been expected. His message was that God's kingdom is announced and lived in the midst of ordinary people, not the heroes, the professionals, or the stars.

The seventy who are sent out are nameless, but that doesn't mean they're unimportant, just used to make a point. I think Luke is saying something important to his little church communities about the nature of the gospel in the midst of their confusion and lostness. These people are looking back to the first generation of Christians and to the stories of the apostles, their brave deeds, and their amazing miracles. But these heroes of the faith are all gone—that era is over and this new generation feels lost and a little adrift.

In the nameless seventy, Luke is saying something about how the gospel indwells a time and a place as well as the nature of the community and its tasks. It is among ordinary men and women, whose names will not be recorded or remembered, that God shapes a future. Contrary to the way we set everything up in the modern West, it will not be from the stars and professionals, the so-called great leaders and gurus, that the direction of God's future is discovered. It will not be through some who get to the top of some proverbial mountain and come down with the directions and solutions that the answers to the questions of what God is up to in the world emerge. It is through the ordinary people of God, the nameless people who never stand on stages or get their photo in the newspaper, that the gospel will indwell their space. This is the strange, counterintuitive imagination Luke seeks to give to these Gentiles and, over the millennia, to us.

Taking Stock

In these last sections I have set a context and presented an argument about how the people of God shaped by a dying Eurocentric church in North America discern what God is up to in this world. I have not given a full response to this question but provided some of the key background elements that must frame our response. Before completing the response to this question, it is helpful to summarize the argument so far and the map that is emerging:

1. God is faithful—but the mission-shaped movement formed by Jesus is bigger than the ethnocentric boxes within which we have tried to contain it.
2. The Spirit is at work in our turbulent world where the categories and maps that once gave us power and control no longer function.[4] The Spirit is breaking the boundaries we have set around the movement of God and calling us out onto a different path.
3. The road onto which we are being called is counterintuitive; it calls us to leave behind our bags filled with methods and models of how to make the church work by creating programs that will attract and catch people. The way of the Spirit involves going on the road as a stranger, needing to receive hospitality from the other. This is a strange inversion of categories and actions—it does not fit with the way of life we have developed as middle-class individualists living in a "make yourself" capitalist culture. Our language house presumes we must be in control of outcomes and methods, but the new language house of Luke 10 takes us in a significantly different direction.

4. There is a link between taking on the nature of the stranger in need and our capacity to discern what God is up to in our world today.

5. In a context of crisis around our identity as Christians in the West, we can discern the shape of God's engagements in the world by becoming a journeying people who enter the ambiguous and vulnerable spaces of mission.

6. It is among the ordinary people of God, the nameless people who never stand on stages or get their photo in the newspaper where God's boundary-breaking future will emerge. The local and ordinary are keys to how churches in North America will reform themselves to join again with the mission of God in the world. This is not to deny the importance of global mission or the connectional nature of our churches, but it is to say that centralized and overarching theories or programs cannot help.

10

A New Set of Practices

Themes of Luke 10

This chapter argues that Luke provides a concrete response to the Gentile Christians for whom he is writing his Gospel. It can be stated in these terms: *the primary way to know what God is up to in our world when the boundary markers seem to have been erased is by entering into the ordinary, everyday life of the neighborhoods and communities where we live.*

Framing this in terms of the way churches function in our time, we can say: *in these times of huge transition where our language houses are being overturned, we will not know what God is up to in the world by huddling together in study groups, writing learned papers, or listening to self-appointed gurus.* The normative means of figuring out answers in the once dominant Eurocentric churches has been to do study and analysis (for example, look at the *biblical* nature of mission, do studies on the essence of the church or the forms of evangelism, and so on), then come up with strategies and programs. Denominational systems have spent huge amounts of money on assessments of what makes for a healthy church or the "seven steps" to turning a church inside out and so forth.

All of these activities, though, are focused on the church and how to make the church work, which is the wrong focus. If one could risk restating Luke's retheologizing in a somewhat radical manner (that may be misunderstood and will be misinterpreted), the point of this text for our Eurocentric churches is: *If you want to discover and discern what God is up to in the world just now, stop trying to answer this question from within the walls of your churches. Like strangers in need of hospitality who have left their baggage behind, enter the neighborhoods and communities where you live. Sit at the table of the other, and there you may begin to hear what God is doing.*

The seventy were sent out into the towns and villages where Jesus would be coming. A part of Luke's response to the question of identity is that discerning what God is doing is tied to entering and becoming present to the people of the neighborhoods and communities where we live. The way this entering is to be done is critical. Those of us who are part of the churches that once held a dominant place in the nineteenth- and twentieth-century religious life of North America are being invited to become like strangers, willing to enter the world of the other to receive hospitality from our neighbor.[1] It seems that in this act of becoming like the stranger and being willing to receive hospitality, we stand a chance of discerning what God is up to. We must explore the meaning of this strange inversion.

Luke is articulating a gospel insight we have largely lost. If these second-generation Christians are in towns and villages all over the Roman world that have little or no idea of the gospel and if these Christians are now confused and anxious about both the speed and depth of the changes in their situation, then part of Luke's response to them is that they are going to rediscover the meaning and shape of the gospel as they enter into the towns and villages where the Spirit has sent them to live.

God's Unexpected Direction

Is Luke 10:1–12 an echo of Jeremiah 29 where the prophet sends a letter from the Lord to the Jerusalem exiles? These are also a people who assumed God would act in certain ways and history would have an outcome that supported their reading of reality. All of that had been shattered by the destruction of Jerusalem and the first temple. Jeremiah's letter instructs the exiles to stop seeking a return to Jerusalem. They are given strange, hugely counterintuitive instructions that would have made little sense to Jewish people—they were to settle in the city of Babylon (its name means "the gate of the gods," implying that this city is *the* place in all the earth where the gods—of the other—come down; one can only imagine the shock of this city on the exiles).

Jeremiah's letter suggests that the only way for these exiles to rediscover their identity as God's people is by dwelling in the very place where they imagined God could never be. This is a stunning reversal of their language house. Nothing could have prepared them for these instructions. Yet there it was—a word from the Lord telling them to embrace and enter this city they had learned to despise.

In a similar manner, is Luke suggesting here to Gentile Christians that they must take their focus off what Jerusalem represented and live among peoples who know nothing of the gospel story? Is this the only way the Christians will be able to answer their questions about what God is doing? Is this what Luke would be writing to us as North American churches, who are confused and disoriented by the massive implosion of our Eurocentric church systems that seemed to work so well for so long? Could it be that this is the Spirit's boundary-breaking invitation to us today? Even while there's still a lot of focus on trying to make our churches work again (making them "healthy" or turning them "inside out"), is the Spirit inviting us to reenter the neighborhoods to discover what God is already doing there? For many of us, this is as shocking and as radical an invitation as the one Jeremiah sent to the captives in Babylon.

Is God calling us to enter deeply into the neighborhoods and communities where we live and/or where our churches are located (the parish system offers some powerful images of what it could mean to be God's people; surely commuting to church is a radical denial of the Incarnation)? Perhaps Luke is suggesting that a primary way of discerning God's plan is when, like the exiles, we reenter the life of the local people, listen to their stories, and love them deeply without feeling the need to "sell" or make a "pitch" or assume we already know what they need and what the gospel ought to look like in this time and place. What would happen if we started in this way rather than with the prearranged designs and assumptions about how church ought to look?

I'm just not convinced anymore we can do this if we are genuinely to enter our local neighborhoods as cross-cultural missionaries. I am not suggesting we don't or shouldn't have traditions or forms around that we will live as Christians. I am not proposing we should throw away our traditions. Not for a moment! These traditions carry with them a rich heritage; they shape us in the ways of the gospel. It is these traditions that give us a language house within which we live, and we can't pretend or deny that this isn't the case. When I am shaped in the language house of the Apostles' Creed; the daily and weekly reading of the Gospel, the Old Testament, and the Psalms; and the regular gift of the Eucharist, I don't enter the neighborhoods and communities where I live as a blank slate. I am who I am because of all these practices of Christian life within a tradition. We shouldn't give these up.

When the exiles found themselves in Babylon, they didn't give up the reading of the Torah or the practice of prayer. They didn't fail to gather at the gate or around the fire and practice midrash. But in this new space that challenged so many of their assumptions about what God was up to, they could discover a way forward and a new way of being God's people only by entering into that place. It was in the entering and the listening that a new discernment, a new language house, a new imagination of what it would mean to be God's people emerged.

Entering the towns and villages where Jesus intended to go was not an aggressive evangelism strategy. Quite the opposite. It was a willingness to enter and be present as the stranger in need of hospitality. Then it was possible to announce the kingdom of God and heal the sick.

A New Text for Our Time

Our language houses are constructed around some primary images. In the twentieth century, for example, when Christians from the Euro-tribal churches thought about the word *home*, their imagination was shaped primarily by the idea of a single-family dwelling with two parents and a number of children. Think of the television series from the seventies through the nineties that primarily depicted this kind of home and family. Even today, when members of these churches are interviewed and asked for metaphors that describe their church, they will more often than not say it is "a caring family"; the idea is similar to the one just described.

This is a powerful language house that comes out of the early nineteenth century and the industrial revolution in England and Europe. But it has little correlation with the reality of North American life today, where the largest percentage of adults lives alone. The ideas of home and family are being radically reshaped, but too often the language house of the churches remains locked into an eighteenth- and nineteenth-century ideal.

The same can be said about the idea of being a people on God's mission. North American churches have lived in a language house that may no longer be adequate or appropriate in terms of the interpretation of a specific text and its meaning for our time. As I wrote in chapter 6, in the nineteenth and twentieth centuries the paradigmatic text that shaped the missionary movement and much of the formation of evangelicalism was Jesus's message in Matthew 28:18–20:

> All authority in heaven and on earth has been given to me. Therefore go and make disciples of all nations, baptizing them in the name of the Father and of the Son and of the Holy Spirit, and teaching them to obey everything I have commanded you. And surely I am with you always, to the very end of the age.

Western Christians took up this text in a time of political, economic, and global expansion and empire building. The language of *power* in that context was one that matched the sense of place, privilege, and requisite authority. There was then a sense of moving out with the right answers for all other peoples because it was through the West that God was shaping the kingdom of God on earth.

This is not to diminish in any way the passionate, courageous work of so many missionaries. It may be that many of these missionaries went out with these notions of power and position, but the most creative ones had learned a different story and a different way. They let go of their power and their sense of position and entered the towns and villages as strangers in need of hospitality so that the gospel could be heard in fresh, meaningful ways.

Overall, however, the interpretation of Matthew 28 came directly out of the sense of power and authority that we in modern, Western culture have. Why did this text become so central to our imagination? Could it have been, again, that for most of the twentieth century, when evangelicalism was in a defensive posture in the culture, this text seemed to endow us with power and authority from God, actually affirming what we already had? We read this text, not as a challenge to go out into all the world, but rather as an affirmation of the power and authority we believed God had given us.

What might it mean to us if this rendering of Matthew 28 can no longer be sustained? What would it mean if we simply no longer have the power and authority to know how and what the gospel must look like among the peoples of a radically changed time and place? Here's the question I want us to explore: *what if God is saying to us that the imperialism, authority, and control that have been behind our use of Matthew 28 are over and that the ways in which we will rediscover the gospel is by becoming a Luke 10 people?* If we believed this, it would transform us from a one-way-dialogue people into those who reenter the conversations with the gospel and our cultures without needing to ask "church" questions all the time. This means a massive culture shift for many churches and their leaders. It involves practicing Luke's description of entering houses.

Entering Houses

Luke 10:1–12 uses the language of a stranger who receives hospitality. It's important here that those who go two by two are the ones who receive hospitality and the gracious goodness of those who live in the towns and villages. Luke repeats the injunction to enter and stay, along with the parallel injunction of eating what is set before them, indicating this entering and eating lie at the heart of his message. Those sent are not to enter a house just for some coffee and conversation; they are to stay in the same house and not jump from place to place.

Several things seem important. First, let us say those being sent, in terms of our situation, represent the churches seeking to make sense of their disorientation, as boundaries are broken and the Spirit is doing things over which we have no control. In this Luke 10 context the location of the "church," if you will, is in the homes and at the tables of the people in the towns and villages, and the stance of the "church" is that of receiving their gracious hospitality (hence, some of the reason for the injunction not to carry extra provisions that make you independent and, therefore, never in need of the hospitality of the other).

Second, this is not, it would seem, a hit-and-run event—there is a strong sense that these disciples stayed with the people for quite some time. Entering the house would not carry the same meaning as it does for us (entering a single-family dwelling). "House" here could be read "household," which meant not only an extended family but an economic unit. The implication is that, in some way, the "church" is to go in such a way that it enters, indwells, and joins the social and economic rhythms of the household (hence, the meaning of the strange comment in verse 7 that the "worker deserves his wages"). This is more than a door-knocking junket to evangelize or invite a neighbor to a special "seeker" service. This is about entering deeply into the life of the other on his or her terms, not your own—"eat what is set before you" (v. 7 NRSV).

Third, these disciples are not to run about from place to place looking for just the right location or just the right kind of people to be with. It would seem that Luke is aware of the belief that the "grass is always greener on the other side of the fence" syndrome, which besets us all. Here, staying put among people is a critical element to being a gospel people and rediscovering the gospel for ourselves. There is no room given here for the language house of meeting with my own kind or being drawn to those who share my values and politics. The neighbors across the street or next door could be from any part of the world today, and chances are they don't share your worldview. This is where we are invited to plant ourselves in the local, making a commitment to the long haul. This is not a hit-and-run mission in an attempt to get our kind of church in place and successful. It seems that for Luke the long view is a prerequisite to engaging the question of what God is doing in the world. This is a very different way of going about discerning God's purposes from the usual Bible study groups in a church that are often comprised of people who all share the same values, have known each other for a long time, and can finish each other's sentences—there is something wildly different happening here.

What does all this say about our congregations and the crisis of identity faced by so many of the Euro-tribal churches in North America? What might be the implications for the kind of transformation that people are eagerly seeking just now? Luke is retheologizing those past decades to invite these Gentile Christians into a different language house about the gospel and God's purpose.

Could it be that the Spirit is inviting us on a similar journey? We, the churches of North America, are being called to reorient ourselves, to be converted all over again in a way that may be more radical than the sixteenth-century reformations. In our day of disorientation and boundary-breaking, we're called to practice becoming like the stranger who needs to be received as a "guest" and welcomed to the table of others who may be very different from us.[2]

Our calling is to enter into their homes (dwell with and among them) and stay with them for quite a period of time without any plans to take off if they or their ways don't suit us. This is going to require radically different ways of thinking about being the church in our day. For one thing, it's going to mean learning how to actually listen to people without making them objects of our ends. It's going to mean a readiness to enter into dialogue with the other, seeking to listen to their stories and conversations in a genuinely human engagement. This is going to feel very strange and disrupting for many Christians, even those in leadership, because it will mean we are no longer in control of the conversation. This kind of engagement will not be about our getting something from the other or deeming the other a potential customer for our "pitch." This leads to another element of what I think Luke may have been communicating to these Gentile Christians whose world was being turned inside out. He wrote that part of Jesus's instructions to the disciples was to eat what was set before them.

Eating and Drinking What Is Placed before Us

Theologian Alexander Schmemann writes:

> Man is what he eats. . . . In the biblical story of creation man is pre-
> sented, first of all, a hungry being, and the whole earth is his food.
> Second only to the direction of propagation . . . according to the
> author of the first chapter of Genesis, is God's instruction . . . to eat
> of the earth: "*Behold I have given you every herb bearing seed . . . and
> every tree, which is the fruit of a tree yielding seed. . . .*" Man must eat
> in order to live; he must take the world into his body and transform
> it into himself, into flesh and blood. He is indeed that which he eats,
> and the whole world is presented as one all-embracing banquet table
> for man. And this image of the banquet remains, throughout the
> Bible, the central image of life. It is the image of life at its creation
> and also the image of life at its end and fulfillment: ". . . that you eat
> and drink at my table in my kingdom."[3]

In the Scripture text, the instruction to stay in the same house is
followed by the phrase, "for the worker deserves his wages" (Luke
10:7). Often this passage has been used to justify paying church workers (again this shows our preoccupation with the internal working
of a church). But what if this phrase has a different meaning? One
can't imagine that these seventy were received into the homes of
townspeople as "Christian workers" and, therefore, given food and
drink! That would be a huge stretch of the text, particularly if Luke
is addressing Gentile Christians in a relatively hostile environment,
which was not particularly welcoming to Christians.

What if these seventy, when they entered into towns and villages,
actually spent time doing manual labor among, with, and beside the
people? This was certainly part of the way Paul functioned during
many of his journeys across the empire. He would regularly find the
local tentmakers and join with them in their work. This was one of
the primary ways he entered into the rhythms of community life.

If this group of seventy were sent out, not as traveling prophets or religious emissaries but, like Paul, to work among the townspeople, we must read this story differently. We have disciples entering into every aspect of the life of the townspeople—working and eating together (remember, at this time people didn't "go to work"; the home and workplace were usually pretty much synonymous, so people would be rubbing shoulders with each other all the time in the "home").

Sitting at the table together would be an opportunity for shared lives and deep communion. It is an honor to be welcomed to someone's table. This is where people talked, as an extended family, about the things in life that mattered. Luke is saying that one of the primary places where disciples should interact with others is at the table of others. Others are the generous hosts; we are those who receive their hospitality. In the midst of these kinds of relationships, we stand a chance of rediscovering the gospel.

This is a strange imagination for us. We live in a time of the continual breakdown of the table as a place where we gather to eat and talk with each other. How rushed our lives have become, represented by the increasing numbers of middle-class people who eat at restaurants or bring home fast food. There are few times when any of us take the time to gather the basic elements of a meal and put together a table where others can sit for a time to talk. This has become an alien way of life for most people.

My wife and I had two young, single women at our table one night. We had cooked supper from scratch as the four of us sat around drinking wine and talking up a storm. It wasn't hard—a bit of risotto with some mushrooms thrown in with grated cheese—simple food that communicated we loved to eat with others and savor the good things of the earth that God has given us. As we sat down, Jane lit a candle and we continued our conversations. The evening went on for a few hours with wonderful conversation. As we sat and listened, we became aware of the struggles these single women experienced, engaging in relationships in a time when we have grown suspicious and fearful of the other. The striking thing about the evening was that these two wonderful people not only thanked us, they told us how rarely they sit at a table with others and just talk.

I don't think this was the case in Luke's world. For early Christians, the table was a natural part of their element. Sitting together at meals was what they did. People gathered around tables in extended households; the stranger was welcomed; the life of the town was shaped around work and table conversation. So Luke is sketching out a primary way, through sitting together at meals, in which these Christians might discover the shape of gospel life in an environment where it made no sense and had no context.

The table is a symbol of where God is taking all of creation. More than a symbol, it is a sacrament that can engage us directly in the life of God. That is, perhaps, one of the reasons the world of modernity has created the belief that fast food, quick meals, and busy lives are the symbols of success—they release us from the sacraments and rhythms that restore and root us in our humanity and personhood. But for humans to flourish, we need to be embedded in such a life.

The table is a symbol of the *eschaton* (God's healed creation in Christ), which has already started among us. These early followers of Jesus were not entering the households as blank slates; they came with the news of God's shalom, their own announcement that God's promised future had come among them. These disciples brought their narrative of God's coming in Jesus to the table.

All of this needs explanation. In the first place, Western Christianity has often equated notions of *eschatology* and *eschaton* with what God plans to do at the end of time. This has certainly been the predominant way it has been interpreted in North America throughout the last century, popularized in such pulp fiction as *The Late Great Planet Earth* and more recently the wildly popular Left Behind series.

What I mean here has nothing to do with this sense of the terms. I use *eschaton* to refer to the ways in which God's future for all of creation in Jesus Christ has already begun with all kinds of foretastes for humanity and creation. In this sense, when we gather for a meal as Christians with others, we are in the presence of God's future. In the midst of our conversations, God's future begins to become materially present. This is what Jesus did with the disciples he met on the Emmaus road as he broke bread with them; it is the picture John gives us from Patmos of what the future will be like—a great banquet where God is here among us in the towns and villages, eating with us in celebration, for "the dwelling of God is with us, and he will live with us forever" (Rev. 21:3).

When I, as a Christian, sit down at someone's table or cook a meal for friends, for me that is a sacrament of the *eschaton* with Jesus present among us. The table is not just a table and the meal is not just food to fill a body with nutrients. The meal is a sacrament that presents and anticipates God's future. Here in Luke, two people enter a house, work side by side with the extended community of that household, and sit to break bread with them at the end of the day, and they talk together. In the midst of these conversations (which require listening to the other) there will lie all the hints and intimations of what God is up to out there ahead of us. This is the word and the world Luke is opening up before us as he retheologizes the events following Jesus's resurrection to address the crisis of identity overcoming the churches.

I believe we are being invited to lay aside all our church questions with all their programs designed to answer our questions about how to reach more people. We are to lay aside our anxious need to say the right words at the right place to get the right decisions and we are to enter the households, work beside people, and sit at tables where we can listen to their stories and enter their dialogue and, perhaps, catch the wind of the Spirit as he births new forms of witness and life in a time grown tired of church conversations.

The Church in Public Space

Luke may be suggesting a radically different location for being the church when the Spirit is breaking our boundaries.[4] What if one of the most important locations for the church isn't so much being centered *in here* as being located *out there*? What if an element of what God is saying to us in this passage is that the nature, meaning, role, and function of the church will be rediscovered only to the extent we learn to discern what God is up to in the interactions with people in the public space and homes of our towns and villages? I'm saying this because, when I read this passage over and over, it strikes me that the answer to the question, Where is the church in this passage? is not in a building filled with people just like us and it's not in a building where regularly scheduled religious meetings occur. It's in the homes of people who are largely outside of those meetings. It's sitting at their tables, listening to their stories, breaking bread with them, and entering into a human dialogue that is not a well-rehearsed sales pitch. This is the location of the church—in the public space.

What if this is the new journey into which God is calling us? This would be a radical shift from our current understanding of church. It's a lot more than training people how to engage others in talking about the gospel or how to move them through steps toward decisions. Can we grasp the implications of what we've become when we have to train people how to have conversations with neighbors or set times aside to talk with another human being? What kind of inhuman world have we created for ourselves, and how has the church managed to accept it and develop marketing skills to manage it? Can we be that far away from the gospel of our Lord that we don't see what we have become? This book proposes a fundamental change in our understanding of how we live as Christians.

Everything has become impersonal today, and with that we have lost the capacity to encounter one another on a human level. By *personal* I don't necessarily mean *individual*. The former has been lost in the latter in our time and that is a great tragedy. We now tend to use *personal* for that which is our own, what is private, but that is not what the word was meant to convey.

When I use the word *personal*, I'm not referring to what is private but to who I am in my relationships with and among particular people at a particular place and time in the world. *Personal* has to do with the kind and quality of person I am, in terms of character and gifts, in relationship with all the people to whom I am connected. Therefore, *personal* is about my connection with others. (The opposite would be some universal type of human being, illustrated by the telemarketer who asks if Mr. Roxburgh is home, so he can offer me a special product that has been developed personally for my needs. In this case I am simply an abstraction, a member of some universal category of people who fit a certain buying profile.)

The personal is grasped directly in real, human, face-to-face engagement, not abstractly as an idea or compilation of the average person. The personal is all about the messiness of relationships over the long term in which knowing and hearing and sharing in the life of the other are critical.

If someone asks me if I know Jesus as my *personal* Savior, in the sense of the word I have just conveyed, I could say, "Yes, yes, *that is who I am!*" But the person would be surprised by my answer, because that's not what is being asked.

I believe Luke 10 is a critical text for our time of dislocation; it challenges the belief that the church is the place for personal self-development and meeting of needs. We can't go on doing church in the ways the Euro-tribal communities of the twentieth century did and we can no longer have as our main concern how to get people into church or the kind of "pitch" we'll use on a potential "seeker" or the "type" of person our focus group study tells us we should go after for a new church plant (shall we go after False Creek Fanny or False Creek Fred?). This is far from the gospel of our Lord.

I'm appealing for the recovery of local and particular ways of calling forth the personal once more in the towns and neighborhoods where we live. For me, this is about dwelling among, working beside, and eating at the table of the men and women who live in our communities, who long for the personal rather than the pitch.

It all sounds so simple and straightforward, so obvious! But it is far from where most of our churches are at this moment. Most have bought into the privatized, individualized culture of the great bazaar and chosen to compete in the market of experiences, using sophisticated sales pitches in their journey to success. If they haven't bought into it, most are trying to find the plan that will get them into the game.

Will this monologue about the church never end? Luke 10 offers an alternative direction—it suggests that the location of the church is in the public space of household, neighborhood, and town. The church will rediscover its life at the table, where bread is broken and stories are told.

Now it is time to turn to the other part of Luke 10—the story and conversations the seventy were directed to share in the households where they stayed. One way of approaching this section of the story is to ask, If the church is to be located *out there* in the public spaces and households of the towns, what is the gospel being asked to communicate? If Luke is addressing a second generation of Christians struggling to reorient themselves in a time and place where the story they have received no longer seems to be making sense, then what is Luke saying to these Christians through this story?

11

Peace, Healing, and the Kingdom of God

Living Out a Subversive Proclamation

They were seen not just as a religious grouping, but one whose religion made them a subversive presence within the wider Roman society.

N. T. Wright

For a lot of Christian leaders the proposals about the location and shape of Christian engagement in an unthinkable world just aren't enough. Suggestions about entering, dwelling, and listening to discern what God is up to just seem bereft of an "edgy" gospel that demands response because it is given with utter clarity. Leaders are unsettled by the proposals outlined in these chapters because they seem empty of the propositions that have to be confessed, the "pitch" that has to be made if one is to get into the "church" conversation. I see these responses in the body language of leaders and hear it in their questions. The perception is that the proposals offered in this book are just not going to get the job done—the job of getting people to confess Jesus as their Lord and Savior and join the church.

I'm not denying the need for men and women to respond to the call of God and the announcement of the kingdom, but something massive is happening to our Euro-tribal churches. A trickle of change that was resisted is becoming a torrent where the boundary-breaking Spirit is radically changing the nature of mission in North America. But let's be clear that experiments in such things as emergent or simple or multisite churches do not change the conversation or the preoccupation. There is nothing formally or imaginatively different about these movements and tactics. Each is a different version of the same old ecclesiocentric, make-the-church-work conversation, the monologue that has been in place for too long.

The Spirit is out there ahead of us, inviting us to listen to the creation groaning in our neighborhoods. Only in the willingness to risk this entering, dwelling, eating, and listening will we stand a chance as the church to bring the embodied Jesus to the world.

I must confess how arduous it is to be met with these "church" questions, realizing that most of those who ask them are still locked into seeking church solutions. Sometimes people will ask if what is being proposed isn't just community development. They mean good works that anybody can do, not really the gospel. Such questions are fundamentally Gnostic and Docetic in nature.[1] I used to argue with such people, but now I know I'm not going to change anyone's mind. How do you paint the pictures that show why, in our time, this is the way God is calling us to rediscover the gospel, not as a marketing strategy but as the hope for all human life and this wonderful creation in which we live?

Uprooting Cherished Assumptions

It is at this point that people ask about my reading of Luke 10, because I have not yet said anything about the "message" the seventy-two were instructed to bring to the households in these towns and villages. Before turning to those issues, one further piece that is implicit in the passage is important to discuss. I'm going to talk about the church for a moment and address the church question that besets leaders so much in our day: how do we reach them to get them in? Of course the question is asked in far more subtle and complex ways than this, but for the sake of our discussion, this way of stating it will do. The typical answer is to turn an inside-looking church into an outside-looking church. (Some call it moving from an internally to an externally focused church, but the discussion in this book should demonstrate that this kind of false polarity is really to miss the point altogether.)

For people asking the question, the church remains the focus of attention. The church is a location and a place where we bring people and where certain things happen. Obviously, there are important elements of being Christians that require us to gather in a place to do certain things, like the sacraments, the recitation of the creeds, formation in Christian practices, and so on. But this has become the limit of what is functionally meant by church for too many Christians and their leadership. It's a place to which we go where certain private, religious experiences take place with like-minded people. In this context it is perfectly understandable that most people, including leaders, simply assume that the gospel is about getting people to know Jesus, and knowing Jesus means coming to church. Church, then, is where you go and it's about certain things you do when you get there.

How might Luke's story be questioning our assumptions about Christian life and the gospel? What hints does it offer as we seek to shape the Christian life today? Rather than assuming we have already read this story many times and figured out what it's about, how might this story "read" us in ways that change our imagination about being God's people? In both Old and New Testaments the Spirit was continually uprooting the basic and cherished assumptions of God's people, overturning their comfortable, manageable lives and the beliefs they had created about God. Luke's two volumes do the same.

A Larger Story

Consciously, Luke sets the narrative of Jesus and the early church in the context of the continuation of the larger story of God's actions that has been going on for a long period of time. Therefore, Luke is committed to being rooted in the narrative memory of Scripture and its anticipation of God's future. For Luke the question of what Jesus is about, and by extension, what the new community is about, can be answered only in terms of continuity with the memory of a specific narrative and within the boundaries of a language house shaped by the Jewish Scriptures and the incarnation, life, death, resurrection, and ascension of Jesus Christ. The Luke text we have examined is not an isolated text to be used for personal edification or some illustration of how to make life work. It's part of a larger story that is, itself, filled with memory and anticipation. Our challenge in letting the story address and read us is that, as heirs of modernity, we are embedded in ways of reading the world that are the opposite of what Luke is communicating. In our time we are driven to excise the past continually and make memory irrelevant so we can make good on the belief that we have started anew with a clean slate. We must be aware of this dynamic if we are to let this story read us instead of blithely using it for our own ends.

For us to grasp the significance of this story, I need to say a few things about the larger narrative in which it is set, namely, Luke's own perception of what is going on. As I have said numerous times, Luke is concerned with what is happening to the growing number of second-generation Gentile Christians who are growing discouraged by the way things are turning out and the darkening clouds of the political and social world around them. In this sense it is an example of pastoral writing. Things don't look that good for his readers. Luke's two volumes focus on issues of social status; the birth stories right at the beginning of Luke's Gospel indicate this tension as well as the keen awareness Luke has of the political world in which these

Christians must now operate. The story of the sending of the seventy must be read within the context of these concerns.

Luke roots the narrative of Jesus in the memory, purpose, and ancient plan of God, presenting Jesus in the image of a prophet like Moses whom God has raised up to bring deliverance.[2] Jesus is, therefore, about the continuation of God's narrative among a people. But Luke shows Jesus to be more than a prophet. He is the prophesied Messiah who comes to announce and demonstrate a great reversal of the order of the world (given the way Luke begins his Gospel, this work of the Messiah is far more than a private, individualistic experience to be worked out within the confines of some "church" world; it is deeply political and social). The poor will have the good news proclaimed to them, the captives will be set free, the blind will see, and the oppressed will be released (Luke 4:18–19). Anyone who has grown up reading the Old Testament or hearing its stories told over and over again will know automatically that these texts are commentaries on the promised shalom of God, which is about his coming reign and the new creation.

Luke is setting the story of the sending of the seventy firmly within the memory and the anticipation of the people of God. The encouragement to these Gentile Christians is that all Jesus began to say and all that has happened to Jesus and these Christian communities are still firmly rooted in what God has been doing from the beginning. This is important because it is telling these young Christians to be confident, even while the picture is confusing. The confidence is not based on the certainty of plans but the Spirit's continuing work of disrupting all things to bring about all that God has promised and done from the beginning.

In Jesus's time, anticipation had been pulled apart—it lay in shattered pieces like painful shards of memory. Since the time of the Babylonian captivity, there had been a diaspora. The memory of that event lived on alongside the Maccabean revolt and the Roman occupation. For most who lived in these towns and villages, the memory of exile continued. Their experience was a failed hope and a fear that little could change. In such contexts people pull into themselves, draw lines around tight little communities, becoming, in our terms, gated and tribalized with a narrow view of themselves and their purposes.

The Essenes were an example; they were the sectarians and communitarians of the time. They believed that if only they could pull the little community of the faithful together long enough, with all the correct practices and habits, they would overcome and God would intervene.

Another group, the Zealots, were a narrow band of radical terrorists bent on disrupting the political and economic nexus of the mighty empire. They felt compelled to act in view of the fact that the old institutions trundled along with ever-increasing regulation as the temple establishment sought to preserve old certainties and normalcy as a way of guaranteeing some semblance of control.

The Pharisees believed that if they could form and model for people a thoroughly righteous way of life, the Messiah would come. These passions, desires, and practices were alive in a swirling environment of expectation and disillusionment. But as it is with all peoples in all times of history, the towns were filled with people who knew of all these movements and just wanted to keep their heads down and get on with life. For most, hope was a luxury they could ill afford in a world that seemed far out of their control and where God seemed unconcerned about the issues they faced.

Jesus: The Story's Fulfillment

In Luke's Gospel, Jesus comes as the bearer of memory and anticipation—the birth narratives point to God's promises. In Luke 4, Jesus opens the scroll to the words of deliverance in Isaiah. There could be no mistaking that he was taking up the promises of God and identifying himself with their fulfillment. The people of the towns where he went saw the healing and miracles as signs of God's kingdom coming among them. Luke is telling these second-generation Christians that in all Jesus did and said, he was signaling that God's promised future had arrived.

In terms of the disciple community Jesus gathered, it is clear that they were not going to function like the disciple bands of other groups. Instead of turning inward, like the Essenes huddled together in expectation of some future tomorrow, Jesus would not allow his disciples to shape themselves around this option (see 9:33 where Peter desires to build three shelters on the Mount of Transfiguration; 9:46–50 where Jesus teaches that to be the least is to be the greatest; and Jesus's description of discipleship that is the prelude to the sending of the seventy in Luke 10). His disciples, unlike the Pharisee groups, don't seem to be focused on keeping all the regulations of righteousness—they would pick grain or heal the sick on a Sabbath. Instead, Jesus gathers and sends out his disciples to announce that God's future has come among them. Luke seems to be making the argument that Jesus's disciples are about continuing the work of their Lord, and Jesus's work is about being sent out, about leaving places of familiarity, control, and security (see Phil. 2:1–11). Luke describes them as being sent like lambs among wolves, as those who take nothing with them on the journey except the words of shalom, the announcement of the kingdom, and the healing of the sick.

What are we to do with this description of a disciple community sent to dwell among people rather than withdraw into closed communities that seek to attract others? What are we to do with this call to live in, with, and among the concrete particularities of people's lives rather than construct predetermined abstract formulas and devices that sort others into formulaic types bearing little connection to any certain individual? How do we answer this question: what is the gospel in this story of the sending of the seventy? Luke 10 addresses such questions differently than do the writings and conversations that have shaped the missional church conversation over the past decade. Today we are seeing the unhappy results of our failure to break out of the church monologue; increasing numbers of books uncritically pick up the missional conversation and apply it to this monologue about the church.

Luke's focus, first, is not that of the "church" but of the gospel as the continuing narrative of the memory and expectation of God's actions in Jesus. Second, Luke is concerned to address these Gentile Christians about the gospel's ongoing encounter with the culture. The engagements we need require the same ordering. We must now shape our conversation by, initially, leaving aside questions of church and begin with the other two sides of the triangle—the gospel and the culture. Only then can we again raise the question of the church. To begin the other way around will only force us back into the default monologue, fortifying the practice of making both the gospel and the culture servants of the church.

This is the point at which a lot of church leaders I know confront me, demanding I pay attention to the fact that the seventy don't just sit at tables or dwell among people; they announce the gospel. They use this fact to argue for the decisionist evangelism so central to and characteristic of contemporary evangelicalism. Here, they argue, is primary evidence for plans and programs to present the gospel to people.

Their critique needs a response. There are three elements to the communication of the seventy: speaking the peace (shalom), healing the sick, and announcing the kingdom of God. Each will be commented on briefly in the light of the argument I am making in this book.

Speak the Peace: Shalom

Each time we walk past someone in the little Italian village where I am writing part of this book, we say either *Buon giorno* (in the morning) or *Buona sera* (in the afternoon). This is a common, everyday

courtesy that neighbors give to one another. In San Diego recently
I was having supper with some friends when a young man came in
and greeted two other men with *Salaam*, which for Middle Eastern
people from a Muslim background is a common greeting that means
"peace from Allah." We give people customary greetings as part of
the social code of a community. In a similar way, there's no question
that speaking the peace (shalom) was a common greeting people
gave to one another all the time in the ancient (and, for that matter,
contemporary) Middle East.

On the other hand, in Luke's Gospel, shalom functions as a lot
more than just a greeting. In the way Luke is writing his Gospel, we
will note that when these disciples of Jesus enter into the towns and
villages, they are among people who know the old stories but have
lost any sense of their vitality. They are getting by and making do
with life, keeping their heads low to avoid trouble from the Romans
and the authorities. When they hear the language of shalom on the
lips of these strangers who are followers of Jesus, it reminds them
of God's promised future. Shalom is the promise of Jubilee and the
rule of God among them. They must have heard this word as a shock
because it would be suggesting that the exile is over.

In the postresurrection narratives of John's Gospel, the story is
told of the disciples (not just the Twelve but a much larger group of
men and women) gathered in an upstairs room with the door bolted
for fear the authorities would come to kill them as they had Jesus
(20:19–23). These were terrified people for whom the story of Jesus
had gone terribly wrong. All bets were off; nothing had turned out
as expected. Confusion and disorientation filled their hearts.

Then Jesus steps into the room, and the text makes it clear he did
not come in through the door. To assuage their shock and terror, he
shows them the wounds in his hands and sides—signs that he was
not an apparition but, in fact, the resurrected Lord. John is focused
on emphasizing the utter materiality and physicality of this moment. The disciples, in John's story, are not projecting their desires

or playing at wishful thinking to compensate for the utter loss of hope. This was Jesus standing before them in his resurrected body. The next points in John's account are crucial.

John is a theologian. Like Luke he is writing a theohistorical account of Jesus and the birth of the church. John weighs his words carefully to construct the point of his story. Those gathered in that upper room had pinned their hopes on Jesus's being the fulfillment of God's promises in the Scriptures. Jesus was to be the one who brought the good news that God's promises were being fulfilled—this is what was involved in the times being filled up and coming to completion.

When, therefore, Jesus stands in that room and says to those gathered, "Shalom," he is not speaking in what might appear to our psychologically driven, modern Western ear as an effort to quell the fear of those in the room. In this word Jesus was picking up the expectations of Israel for the shalom (kingdom, reign, rule, future) of God. In this word Jesus was announcing that the promises of God's coming reign are now being fulfilled in his resurrected presence.

This is the same meaning of the word *shalom* Luke is using in 10:5–6. When the seventy go to the towns and villages, they are announcing that God's future has come in Jesus. The seventy announce good news, but what is the nature of this good news? One suspects that for at least some in those towns and villages, it must have been a terrifying announcement they did not want to hear in the midst of empire occupation. The healing of the sick was, itself, a sign that in these followers of Jesus the promised kingdom of God was coming. Exile was over!

The Kingdom of God

The seventy also announce and demonstrate the kingdom of God. Three times in this brief story the kingdom of God is mentioned. Again the question is what the announcement of the reign of God would have meant for the men and women in the towns that Jesus visited. To understand its significance, first, we need to understand that for these people the exile, which took place in the sixth century BC, was not over. They continued in exile from the promises of God. Second, they had the memories of a kingdom where their own David and Solomon ruled the world. This kingdom had been snatched away. Finally, they are under the control of another king and another empire. The Pax Romana was a bitter reminder of a lost past and continuing exile.

Jesus comes to bring and embody God's promises. This is what happens in Nazareth in Luke 4. Luke also portrays Jesus as a form of second Moses and so identifies him as the one who comes to release the captives. When the seventy announce the kingdom of God, they are proclaiming that in Jesus captivity is coming to an end and a new exodus is about to begin. The enlivening conviction shaping these early Christians from the beginning was the profession that the kingdom of God had drawn decisively near in Jesus. Their focus was the kingdom in Jesus. In Luke 10 we are confronted with the fact that any announcement of this kingdom in the name of Jesus results in conflict of major proportions—shaking off the dust and Sodom are not tame images.

Implications for Now

Luke's focus, therefore, is so very different from that of Euro-tribal churches at the beginning of the twentieth century who are trying to find tactics to fix and adjust their churches in the midst of massive boundary-breaking. Luke is not all that interested in getting a right model for being the church or coming up with a clear delineation of what it means to be the church. He's interested in the continuity of a story that was going forward long before Pentecost. It is a story about the reign of God that Jesus announces, embodies, and fulfills. The end to which all of history is moving can now be clearly seen by all (Eph. 1:9–11), and it will not be seen in the mighty or in empires or in abstract ideas like freedom and truth, but in ordinary, obscure people who broke bread, drank wine, and gave themselves away for the sake of the world.

In this sense the seventy were practicing eschatology; they were announcing something longed for and now present—they were announcing that the firstfruits of a restored Israel were present and that all the promises that had been given to Israel were now continuing under radically new circumstances in Jesus. Therefore, we cannot understand what Jesus is up to or what was happening when Luke penned this story, without first living inside this wider story. It is clear that it is about the mission of God, not the needs of church members. It was about the contagious joy a person has when inside the one, true story about people and the whole direction of the world.

The announcement of the kingdom meant Jesus is the bearer of the subversive memory that is full of anticipation. Our work is rekindling the environment in which this subversive story will once again enter our churches, leading to questions about almost every assumption on which they have been constructed over the past century. This can be done only by risking this "going without baggage" and entering the everyday lives of ordinary people in our neighborhoods.

I watch my grandchildren emerging into life, developing language and habits as they live among us, their parents, grandparents, aunts, and uncles. Adam, Owen, Maddy, Ben, and Ethan are in and out of our home. We play with them on our knees, read to them, and carry them sleepily to bed. They know that, when they come to Grandma and Granddad's house, there are predictable events and experiences they can anticipate. They have a sandbox, a tree to climb, a special cupboard filled with their toys, "fishy crackers" to eat, iTouches and iPhones on which to play "Doodle Jump," and on and on.

Throughout the year Jane takes copious photos of them through the seasons at play and in special events we do together. Just before

Christmas she creates a story around the pictures that tells of who we are as a family and what we have done together. When it's completed, it goes off to a printer, and on Christmas day each family receives its yearly book. We are into our fifth or sixth edition at this point. What is happening to our grandchildren in these growing experiences is that they are being nurtured inside a story. It is the story of this family and its antecedents that will shape them.

We are weaving a narrative just as our parents and grandparents did to and with us. I think it is all much harder these days because there are so many more competing and beguiling stories to capture and color our worlds. It gets harder because ours is a culture that has formed us to believe that the stories are all intended to make us the center of meaning and fulfillment. That is how it has been from time immemorial until very recently when all stories seem to get liquefied in a complex universe of apparent multiple choice and endless self-creation.

Too often this is what has happened to the story of Jesus and the coming of the kingdom. Churches are so focused on themselves because ours is a culture whose language house tells us we are to be focused on ourselves, that the story of Jesus is lost. Yet the role of a local church is to form a people around the presence of God among us in Jesus Christ. This has always been accomplished in two primary ways: first, through worship that directs us to the mystery, otherness, and wonder of God's grace and love toward us in Jesus Christ; and, second, through catechesis, formation in practices of Christian life. These must always be at the center of Christian communities. These are the essential ingredients for participating with the God of mission. In so many ways each of these ways of life, the language house of worship and formation, have been lost to us. This is the reason the boundary-breaking Spirit is decentering and marginalizing the Euro-tribal churches of North America. God is doing something far bigger than tribal survival or measuring all things by certain sixteenth-century events in Europe.

The Spirit is breaking apart a form of church that took shape in the Protestant West from the sixteenth century forward. There are all kinds of material reasons that can be given for this, from falling birth rates to secularization theories to a new globalizing pluralism and so forth. But if Luke were writing his two volumes today, he would probably eschew the sociopolitical reasons, not because they are unimportant but because they miss the point of it all. God is on the move. The kingdom is so much bigger than our little, tribal cultural enclaves, and the world is in crisis. The Lord of creation is out there ahead of us; he has left the temple and is calling the church to follow in a risky path of leaving behind its baggage, becoming like the stranger in need, and receiving hospitality from the very ones we assume are the candidates of our evangelism plans. Luke's retheologizing would say that the only way we can understand and practice again this kingdom message is by getting out of our churches and reentering our neighborhoods and communities. This is where we will discern God's future, not in our vision and mission statements or the arrogant need to start a movement in our own image. This is a time for a radical shift in the imagination and practices of our once dominant Euro-tribal churches.

PART 3

A NEW LANGUAGE HOUSE

12

Rules for Radicals

The Contours of a Method

How might a local church begin to live out the implications of this book? These final two chapters sketch a direction. We have entered a new space; we're walking in new territory in a time when so much is unknowable. It's not possible to lay out a big strategy or a detailed plan. There is much to be done in testing and experimenting. We need to gather and tell stories of those communities of Jesus that are risking moving back into or awakening to their neighborhoods, and we need to hear the ways in which God is going ahead of us.

These are early days. The majority of our leaders still remain firmly locked into the language houses of tending to and shaping everything in terms of the church and its success. That's what they have seen and how they are trained in seminaries and Bible schools. Recently I asked a denominational leader what she thought was the greatest challenge facing the clergy and local church leaders for whom she had oversight. She went down the usual list of contenders, then paused and said, "No, none of these are the real issues. It's not about more training or getting them more time away from administration or even more skills in certain areas. As important as these may be, they all pale in comparison to what I think we are really facing. When I listen to my leaders with their plans and visions, at the bottom of it all, they are still working at trying to get people into their churches and make them successful. It's not that this is wrong; it's not the point. The real challenge we face is how to transform the imagination of our leaders for them to see it's not about getting their churches filled; it's about joining with what God is doing in the world." Then she acknowledged how difficult it is to change this default imagination.

Taking the Journey

There is no simple, painless method of change. The risks involved in practicing Luke 10 are high; the story is full of warnings about this all along the way. The story makes no pretense of offering easy answers. Those late-first-century Gentile Christians were being challenged to let go of a deeply entrenched imagination and trust that God was up to something radically outside anything they had come to expect. The history of the first several centuries of the church suggests that at least some of them went outside their assumptions and language houses without baggage and entered the towns (neighborhoods and communities) of the empire because the empire, if only for a moment, bowed its knee to Jesus. Ours is a similarly arduous, risky, and uncertain journey. This chapter will outline a series of proposals for taking that journey. The final chapter will offer a specific way in which any local church can go about practicing Luke 10.

The Rules

The title of this chapter is taken from a book written many years ago by a man of radical convictions about how to form communities of hope. Saul Alinsky was born of Russian Jewish immigrant parents in Chicago in 1909. He understood what it meant to live on the edge, to struggle with how to live within shifting language houses that often put the powerless in ever more perilous situations. Without endorsing his political ideology, we can see in Alinsky a man who understood that imaginations are changed through the development of rules rather than the piling up of knowledge, information, and metrics. He developed a set of simple rules ordinary citizens could follow to address their sense of powerlessness and discover that among them they had the resources and imagination to create a different future for themselves. Beneath Alinsky's rules lay a rock-hard conviction that, in giving ordinary men and women a set of simple rules, they would be able to change their situation and overcome those who had seemingly unbreakable power over them. It is this conviction about the ways ordinary people, in the ordinariness of their context, transforming their environment, that undergirds the steps outlined in this chapter.

If the boundary-breaking Spirit is out ahead of us in our neighborhoods and communities, it will be through simple rules, not complex plans or the visions of leaders, that we will see God's future emerge among us. Along the lines of Alinsky's "rules for radicals," which have shaped the imagination of all kinds of reformers right up to the present day, I have adopted the spirit of his insight to develop ten rules that any leader and local church can follow if they want to enter the way of Luke 10:1–12.

1. Go Local

The first basic rule is extremely simple to articulate but not so easy to do—go local. This means that the focus of a local church and its leaders needs to be on two things. First, the focus must be on the ordinary lives of the people of a local congregation through which the Spirit is shaping a new future. Second, the focus must be on the local contexts as the venues for discerning and engaging that future.

As we have seen, we discover what God is doing in the world and what it means to be the church as we move back into the neighborhood. This is both a simple and radical proposal. It's radical because for many of us there is little connection between where we live, where we go to church, and what it means to be a Christian. That's the tragic state of Christian life in North America. Christian leaders regularly tell me that they have no time to know who lives in their neighborhood and, besides, they tell me, neighborhoods are a thing of the past; that's the "old" way of thinking; we don't live like that today. A radical way we can re-form Christian life in our time is by the simple decision to reconnect with our neighborhoods, by asking what God is doing there. If you want to recover the sanity of your life and that of your family in deeply Christian rules, reconnect and reenter your neighborhood.

It is at this point that a lot of people agree with this idea of going local but they wonder about the focus on neighborhood when we live in what they call a "networked" world. I have written about this before so will only summarize the reasons here.[1] Briefly, the problem with the "network" idea is the same problem faced and not addressed by too many local churches—homogeneity. Look at the networks to which you belong! Chances are most of them are comprised of people in the same economic, social, and ethnic group as you and they generally share the same political and religious views. The boundary-breaking Spirit is interested not in re-creating homogeneous Euro-tribal churches but in calling forth local communities that manifest the new creation in a globalized world. Today most neighborhoods are increasingly ethnically mixed and represent the new religiously pluralist society North America has become. The Spirit is calling us to go local in such neighborhoods rather than running back to our homogeneous networks.

What we need here is to develop habits and rules in our local churches that help our people move back into their neighborhoods (they are already there but too often, emotionally and in terms of time or focus, they are hardly present to the neighborhood) as the focal location of Christian life and rule. Instead of building local church life around church programs (to which we are supposed to invite people to come) let's make the focus the neighborhood and community, then turn the local church into the center of formation for the equipping, sending, and resourcing of their people in the local.

2. *Leave Your Baggage at Home*

Leave your baggage at home is a profoundly world-changing instruction. We have discussed it at length in previous chapters, so I will only summarize here. More than anything else this is a gospel plea for the humanization of our relationships with others, rather than seeing the people of our neighborhoods as potential objects for our church marketing strategies (often called evangelism or outreach). It is also a plea to leaders to set down their need for vision statements or the hormonal drive to create some kind of major "movement." These activities are about "baggage"; they leave us in control of relationships because we are predetermining what they need to accomplish as well as creating barriers that prevent us from being surprised and hearing the new things the Spirit might want to do outside our vision, mission, and strategic plans.

Leaving your baggage behind means that the local church learns together how to become like "strangers" who receive the hospitality of the people in the community. This is really learning how to have basic, simple, ordinary human relationships with the people in our community without any other strategy or intent.

Again the reactions to this proposal are plain and are raised with great regularity: "All this is good. It sounds like social work or good community development, but when do we get to the gospel?" As discussed in the previous chapter, this response betrays a basic Gnosticism with its false polarities that separate the good news of God in Jesus from the basic indwelling of life described here. Furthermore, it conveys a massive lack of imagination and a failure to understand the ways in which our people are shaped from within the Christian narrative. Lurking behind these kinds of questions is the assumption that when I sit at the table of my neighbor and enter into his or her world in dialogue, I am some kind of blank slate, who brings nothing with me. This is patently absurd but it is the assumption in the question.

At the risk of repetition, let me say that, when I sit with my neighbors to listen and enter their stories, I am there as one who is shaped week in and week out by the liturgies of worship with the confessions of faith, the reading of Scriptures, and the affirmations of forgiveness. I am formed weekly by the Eucharist as I kneel to receive the bread and wine. I can no more sit at the table of my neighbor as a blank slate than I can deny I am a male.

The problem here is that most of our worship and church experiences don't form us in the language house of the Christian narrative. The point about going without baggage is the stance, the spirit, and the attitude with which I am present in the neighborhood. It is the opposite of planned outcomes and predetermined strategies to get people turned into something I want. But that is not to deny the presence of the Spirit in the midst of this being sent. He is right there, present in the conversations and working in the spaces between our conversations in ways that will surprise me because I have come as a stranger in need of hospitality, in need of receiving, without any tactic that turns my neighbor into an object of my goals. This is the amazing place where God does things we could never imagine.

3. Don't Move from House to House

The instruction not to move from house to house is pretty straightforward—settle into the neighborhood, bloom where you're planted, and stop imagining there's a better place or the grass is greener on the other side of the fence. In other times this was known as the rule and vow of stability; that is, stay where you are and be present to the people among whom you live in your neighborhood.

We have been a society that moves about, often grasping after upward mobility or the lie that we need more space to attend to the individualistic needs of our children and ourselves. All this movement cuts us off from being present in a neighborhood. Too many of us spend so much time running from church meeting to church meeting or some demand or another that we have almost no time for the kind of being present in a community we will need to cultivate if we are to indwell our neighborhoods.

Make no mistake about this call to stability and place—in twenty-first-century suburban society it is radically countercultural. If there is anything that attracts increasing numbers of people to investigate the new monasticism, it is this elusive call to stay in one place, love where you are, and take a vow of stability. There could be nothing more powerful as a witness to the alternative story of God's future than Christians who take this vow to stability and make their own neighborhoods the primary location of their lives. The implication of Luke 10 is that we will not discern what God is doing in our society until we take on the rule of stability. Obviously one cannot legislate or program this way of life in a local church. The place to begin is with simple, small experiments among some of the people of a local church as will be described in the last chapter. But, frankly, this reimagining the nature of local church life will not happen unless those in primary leadership live this life by example.

4. Eat What Is Set before You

Several years ago I was in China with a group of North Americans. Our hosts wanted to share their food with us. They had spent a lot of time thinking through how to share with us their experience of cooking and eating. Most of the food was very foreign to a North American palate in terms of the elements used and the ways it was cooked. Several of the people in the group simply would not eat the food set before them. I will never forget one person leaning over to tell me she was desperate to find a McDonald's and have a decent American meal.

Recently I was in South Korea for the first time, being treated to Korean food. The wonderful people with whom I was meeting were eager to take me to restaurants where, awkwardly sitting cross-legged on floor cushions, we delved into the delights of Korean cuisine. One evening in Pushan I ordered a plate of squid, not aware how proud these people were to serve the freshest of seafood. When the plate came, I picked up my chopsticks and was ready to eat until I saw the small pieces of squid moving on my plate. The squid was so fresh the nerves in each piece kept them moving about.

Delighted Korean friends watched me, wondering what I would do. As I ate the squid, I could tell that something had changed. My friends realized I was someone who wanted to meet them in their world. They were willing then to welcome me not just to the table but to a conversation.

The rule of eating what is set before us is about our readiness to enter into the world of the other on his or her terms rather than our own. We are all shaped inside the sounds, tastes, and perspectives of our own small worlds and have come to expect we can stay inside these shells of comfort getting our own needs met. This rule calls us to a different way of being with people. It involves a readiness to be present with someone else in ways that meet them in their context and environment. Again, this would be a radical shift in Christian life and witness if we began to find some simple ways of practicing this way of life in the neighborhoods where we live as God's people.

5. *Become Poets of the Ordinary*

The rule to become poets of the ordinary will be, at first, the work of leaders as they help people reflect on what is happening in their neighborhood encounters. The poet is one who listens to the stories that lie beneath the stories people tell and gives voice to the music beneath their words.[2] The poet is the one who, in such listening, offers ways in which people can connect this music to a larger movement, to a bigger story. The work of being a poet addresses the anxiety of the modern-day Gnostics who ask, "When do we get to the gospel?" As we enter the local, stay in that place, and learn to eat what is set before us, we find ourselves entering the stories and hearing the music of the other in ways we could never do if we relied on programs or the calculation of where someone is on a scale of readiness for the gospel. It is in the safe space of table and conversation that we hear the rhythms and stories of our neighbors. This is the context in which we can become poets of the ordinary who connect people's stories with God's great story.

This is not, however, a one-way street as if we are simply using the conversation as a tactic so we can interject the gospel. Poets tell stories and connect stories. They point and suggest and evoke. Jesus continually engaged people in this way. Whether he was with the woman at the well or Nicodemus late at night, Jesus was a poet listening to their stories and then evoking in them disquieting questions because he connected their stories with something in God's story that caught their attention but didn't give a solution.

The other side of being a poet is that we get changed in the process as well. As we listen to the story of a neighbor, we too become shaped by that story and start to see that God's story doesn't only connect with the neighbor but it also challenges and, often, questions the ways we have automatically assumed what the gospel is all about. This is what happens to Peter when he listens to Cornelius. It happens to Saul as he's rushing down the road to Damascus or sitting in a circle of tentmakers in the markets of Corinth or Rome or Ephesus. As a poet of the kingdom, Paul must have been continually having his world rearranged and his imagination of what God was doing reshaped by these encounters around tables and amid the daily lives of people.

6. *Move the Static into the Unpredictable*

A simple but powerful rule of formation is to move the static into the unpredictable. Too often in our churches the rhythms of life have become static and terribly predictable in terms of programs, habits, and attitudes because people have become ingrown. To get at this hardening of a local church's arteries, leaders need to find ways of creating some disruption. Of course too much disruption will lead to system breakdown and responses of anger and resistance. But too little disruption will leave everything as it is. The skill here is knowing what is too much and what is too little in a specific local church.

There is no formula for this; it's an art that involves listening well to a congregation to hear the Spirit-created desires people have to disrupt the static. It is about being awake to those moments when the unpredictable turns up and we know how to invite people to ask new questions about what is happening rather than just trying to fix everything.

Illustrations of this abound. One local church is experiencing a growing level of anxiety because it is aging and losing young adults and young families. People don't know what to do about it. They are afraid to give voice to this anxiety because they don't want to disrupt the static. These are good people. They are not closed to wanting God's future but they have been formed in a world of church programs that once worked yet no longer do. They have also been raised not to express their concerns or rock the boat. All of this has created an environment where anxiety is present but it's pushed underground by the power of the static.

People are nostalgic for a past when the church had kids all over the place and the now-aging members were young couples, volunteering and running programs. When they are able to voice their anxieties, several things happen. First, they place blame. The preaching is boring, the youth program is in bad shape, and so forth. Second, their solutions are in terms of the static world they know. They suggest, for example, revamping the youth program or setting up intergenerational meals to connect with each other. These answers involve doing more of the same, putting in place what once worked when they were much younger.

These are not people without imagination, but they are locked into the static. What should one do as a leader? Disrupt the static and create spaces for the unpredictable! How? Why not, for example, help people give voice to their anxieties? Be like a poet and help them name what they're feeling. Then, recognizing that these good people will keep coming up with the same old programs as solutions, offer a proposal. Invite some of them to go and talk with their nonchurch-going grandchildren about their lives and what is important to them. Help these people write "appreciative inquiry" questions to ask young people in the community. (Appreciative inquiry is a method of asking open-ended questions that invite people to share their stories.) Then come back together, share the responses, and assist people to hear the voices beneath the words in these conversations. In the midst of such interaction, people start naming the fact that the old programs and solutions aren't going to make a dent in reaching young people and young families. This is when the unpredictable emerges; it comes from the people themselves and their conversations.

7. *Listen People into Speech*

The illustration above of moving people out of their static is an example of "listening people into speech." The people in the illustration knew that something was amiss in their church life but didn't know how to give voice to what it was. Because of this they would express themselves in terms of programs needed in the church or the ways leaders needed to improve what they were doing. None of these proposals came close to what was actually needed. The problem was that the static life of the church closed down the capacity of people to connect with and give voice to what was happening inside them; all they could speak were the change proposals.

Listening into speech involves the skill of creating the spaces where people can give voice to their anxieties, hopes, and fears, as well as the music that lies beneath. This is the reason leaders need to be more like poets than program designers, more like creators of the unpredictable than fixers of the static. Some of the process outlined in the illustration shows how to listen people into speech. When people feel it is safe to give voice to their unspoken hopes and stories and these are brought into conversations with the biblical narratives, we start to hear the life of the Spirit among us.

This listening into speech is what those of us in local churches have to learn so that we can sit at the table of neighbors and hear their stories. If this is where the Spirit is at work—out ahead of us—then we need to become a community of people who are giving this gift to one another. Then we will be able to give it to people in our neighborhoods and communities. One of the primary roles of leaders in this context is making it a priority to keep listening their people into speech.

8. Experiment around the Edges

The temptation of many leaders remains the need to fix problems with big strategies, more programs, and importing programs from outside. Instead of defaulting to these predictable, manageable solutions that have the appearance of addressing challenges, create experiments around the edge.[3]

In the illustration above, the leader didn't respond to the anxieties of church people by creating a new youth program or setting up a series of cross-generational meal events. Instead, this leader invited people to do some simple experiments in listening others into speech.

The experiments gave people their own sense of empowerment; they were doing something for themselves, as well as creating the listening spaces where they could start to ask different kinds of questions. This process created new energy among people. It resulted in their willingness to try some experiments in connecting with youth in their community as well as simply asking other churches why they had so many youth. These actions created a new space for thinking about how to be God's people in a changed world.

Often the problem is not that people are resistant to change; it's that they haven't been given the chance to imagine alternatives or empowered to do their own work of discovery through experimenting.

9. *Cultivate Experiments, Not BEHAGS*

This rule—cultivate experiments, not BEHAGS—builds on and is a subset of rule number eight. One of the primary blockages to releasing the imagination of the people in a local church and having them enter their neighborhoods is this deep-seated need of leaders to come up with a big plan or the right model to make the church work.

A BEHAG is a Big Hairy Audacious Goal. It is the knee-jerk reaction of leaders to come up with something really big that catches the imagination of people and gets them all involved in making a difference. The problem with these big visions is that, first, they don't last; second, they don't change anything; and, third, they create disappointment and loss of hope as, several years on, leaders come up with yet another BEHAG.

This rule moves in two directions. First is the spiritual determination to resist BEHAGs, seeing their source for what it is—the anxiety-driven need of leaders to be seen as in charge (or the hormone-driven passions of younger leaders who believe they can have a wonderful plan for everyone else's life). Second is the determination to focus attention on moving back into the neighborhoods. As we listen people into speech, we can cultivate simple, often small, experiments.

10. Repeat Rules One through Nine Over and Over Again

Finally, keep repeating these rules over and over again. The plain fact of the matter is that real change in the culture of a local church takes place as we practice these simple rules as a way of life. If you want to see a deeply transformative movement of your people in the neighborhoods and communities where they live, start to practice these rules, remembering that things begin to change when we repeat the rules over and over again.

Creating a Luke 10 way of life in and through our local churches takes time and is about learning simple habits and rules. It is not big ideas and piles of knowledge that change the culture of a people; it is doing what Jesus does in Luke 10:1–12. He sends out a group of seventy disciples into the neighborhoods and communities to live by some simple rules. In so doing he creates a new language house for mission in the local.

Luke is working with these stories to assist Gentile Christians faced with a crisis of identity to grasp how they might reorient themselves in a new space. That reorientation involves taking on counterintuitive practices and rules for being God's people. The same calling is being laid on the once dominant Euro-tribal churches now struggling to understand what has gone wrong and still trying to fix it by revamping the same old church-focused programs. The boundary-breaking Spirit will have none of it. The Lord has left the temple, picked up a new set of wheels, and is already ahead of us out there in our neighborhoods and communities.

13

Beginning the Journey

Some Practical Steps

This final chapter proposes a way a local church can join with this movement of the Spirit. Already a growing number of experiments are taking place in many parts of North America. Some of us are starting to collect the stories of how Christians are moving back into the neighborhood and starting to learn a Luke 10 way of life. Where might a local church begin this strange new journey? In Edmonton, Alberta, Howard Lawrence has been quietly and gently cultivating this way of life with his family in their neighborhood. In Eagle, Idaho, Mark Priddy has been doing this for some years already. In Denver, Colorado, local churches are seeking to practice this way of life. In San Diego, Chicago, Atlanta, and the Bay Area around San Francisco, my colleague Mark Lau Branson and I have met with hundreds of Christians to share with them some of the things we're learning about shaping Luke 10 types of communities. Under the radar, pioneers are already experimenting in a Luke 10 way of being church in their local context.

Some, misunderstanding what it's all about, are already trying to franchise some kind of "moving back into the neighborhood" program without any real sense that this is about cultivating from the bottom up in the local.

More than twenty years ago I wrote a book for InterVarsity Press called *Reaching a New Generation*, describing the tectonic shifts that would reshape the relationship between Christian life and the culture of North America. The intervening years have shown that these shifts continue to rearrange the nature of church life for us all. In the latter part of that book, I reflected on many of the efforts to renew, re-form, and reshape the church to engage this emerging context. Thinking ahead and imagining what it might mean to be God's witnessing people, I wrote these words:

> Today's church is in crisis. Its renewal requires far more than liturgical change or doctrinal correction. Focusing on new structures is . . . not an adequate response. The tectonic plates of Western culture are shifting. As modernity is questioned and parts rejected, the church is also questioned and marginalized. . . . Despite all our protestations the church in North America remains focused on itself. Until this is changed, evangelization will continue to look like forays into the world in order to recruit members for our clubs.[1]

I concluded the book with a picture of the way ahead, which was not about bigger and bigger churches located out of neighborhoods or more churches effective at getting other Christians into their buildings. I saw a different kind of movement involving thousands and thousands of lights being lit in neighborhoods and communities across the continent, as God's people *moved back into their neighborhoods* to rediscover that God was already ahead of them creating and calling forth that which is new. Local churches can be a part of this movement. In fact they are the key to the creation of such a movement. In this light we have developed a set of proposals for guiding local churches into Luke 10 engagements with their neighborhoods. This chapter outlines the elements of the process for those eager to get started on the journey.

This outline presents a series of steps your local church can take to initiate several groups for reconnecting with their neighborhoods, learning to ask the questions of what God might be up to already in the neighborhood, discerning where they might join with the Spirit, and then reporting back to the church in ways that will invite others to join this journey.

Step 1: Prepare the Local Church

Communicating with the Board

One of the most important first steps in initiating a Luke 10 life in your local church is to get your board connected so they understand what it all means and how people can get involved. You want to ensure good buy-in from the church's leadership so that key people feel ownership of the process.

Communicating with the Church

You want to create a climate of invitation and conversation so that people feel welcomed into a process of moving back into the neighborhood. Don't just announce decisions that have already been made or pass out information sheets and expect people to buy in. At the beginning it's very important to work at building ownership across the church rather than announce some top-down decision about creating a few groups who will be looking at how the church might reengage the neighborhoods where its people live. Giving people ownership, getting them involved, and keeping them informed are critical from the beginning. Let people know what you're thinking and provide a rationale that helps them understand what it means to be God's people in the neighborhood. This might involve doing the following:

1. Teach and have conversations with people in the church about what it means to move back into the neighborhood, why this is important, and what would be the benefits to the local church.
2. Identify people who can tell brief stories about being present in their neighborhood. Provide multiple times for this sharing of stories.
3. Invite input and responses as you practice listening to the people of your church.
4. Use biblical texts in your preaching around the metaphor of neighbor; see, for example, the parable of the good Samaritan (Luke 10:25–37) as well as Luke 10:1–12.
5. Set up a brief communications workshop so that any who would like more information or want to ask questions can do so. You'll be surprised at the people in a local church who know the neighborhood really well and want to make connections for you. The more of this kind of involvement that gets created in the church, the greater your learning, the richer the discoveries, and the more ownership there will be.

Forming Teams

It's important to identify the people who will form a number of neighborhood teams. Establish patterns for gathering together during the process and practicing the spiritual discipline of listening to Scripture. Here it is important to share basic information about what's involved and provide potential team members with a guidebook, such as the *Moving Back into the Neighborhood* workbook, that outlines a step-by-step process with expectations and timelines.[2]

It may take several months of preparation to form these groups. People will need lots of time for questions and dialogue to understand what is involved in moving back into the neighborhood and its meaning for being God's people in their context. Your goal, by the end of a three-to-six-month period, is to establish a couple of teams within specific neighborhoods who will meet together for a six-to-eight-month period to follow the steps outlined below.[3]

Step 2: Develop New Eyes for Your Neighborhood

Moving back into the neighborhood is about learning to see our community with a fresh set of eyes. This step looks at the story of Jesus's healing a blind man. At first, the man sees people, but they look like trees; Jesus touches the man's eyes again, and he sees people.

We may not be physically blind from birth but we can easily take our neighborhoods for granted and stop seeing what is going on there among people. An important part of joining with God in mission-shaped life is learning to see again with fresh eyes, to wake up to the fresh and not-so-obvious ways God is present. How might we learn to see our neighborhood through God's eyes and become detectives of God's life in our neighbors and the activities of the streets where we live? To do this, people start to practice:

1. Dwelling in the Word around Luke 10:1–12 each time they meet together.
2. Learning to walk through their neighborhood and ask new questions about what is happening there. They would keep simple notebooks reflecting on questions like the following:
   - Without asking someone else, can I provide the first and last names of the people who live beside (or above and below) me?
   - What can I describe about their lives that can be known only by someone who has been inside their home?
   - What are some of the God-shaping longings and/or questions that currently shape their lives?

Step 3: Teach Radical Neighborliness

People ask why we bother with this idea of the neighbor and the neighborhood when so many of us live in what we call a *connected* world, where we meet friends online or travel across town or to another part of the country to meet them. Most of us just drive in and out of our neighborhoods; at the most we sleep and have meals there. Surely there are more important places to live kingdom life in this postmodern world. Isn't the neighborhood just a throwback to some other time? Shouldn't we be focused on the "now" and the contemporary, rather than on these old forms of life?

If you ask a random group of people about who they know on their street, or in their complex, the answer would probably be similar to the one Steve S. gave. He said, "I've lived on this street for three and a half years and I know the names of a couple people; that's about it." Another person put it this way: "I have 470 'friends' on Facebook but don't know anyone where I live." Neighborhood is a critical place where, as Christians, we can live, witness, and be a mission.

This step helps people move from the step of walking around their community to connecting with the stories of some people where they live. To do this groups will:

- Talk together about the parable of the good Samaritan, asking new questions about who is our neighbor.
- Share with each other what they've been discovering in some of their walking around the neighborhood.
- Share some "first" stories about the neighborhood with one another.
- Plan a neighborhood BBQ or something that might gather people.

Step 4: Map the Neighborhood

As people walk around, they start to develop fresh eyes and see what they may have taken for granted before. A helpful way to develop new eyes is to draw your own map of your neighborhood and share with one another the stories of what you're seeing. This mapping helps you discover what you may have not seen and appreciate what is actually happening every day that you have been missing. It helps you learn to ask new kinds of questions about your community. In this step groups build on the work of the previous steps as they:

- Continue to dwell in the parable of the good Samaritan.
- Begin looking carefully and then drawing their own neighborhood maps.
- Share their maps with one another.
- Discuss new questions and observations about their neighborhood.
- Identify gathering places in the neighborhood and discuss how to connect with them.
- Share stories while practicing hospitality with some of the people in the neighborhood.

Step 5: Listen to Neighborhood Stories

In connecting and building relationships in the neighborhood, people in the groups now want to listen to the stories shaping the lives of their neighbors. This is critical to hearing what God might be up to around us. Through stories we make fresh discoveries about our community as we listen without presuming, concluding, or trying to develop strategies for getting them to do or become something. This might sound counterintuitive, but it is important to realize that by listening carefully we may be able to discern where we can join with what the Spirit is doing in our communities. This practice of joining with the Spirit (remember the Luke 10:1–12 passage) will give us the capacities to discover fresh ways of being the church in and for our communities. In turn the church will grow and be transformed in ways that can't be imagined or predicted at the outset.

Often people ask how they go about listening to and discerning the stories of their community. Here are some things to keep in mind in terms of examples of where people gather:

- Young moms may meet in certain spaces and carry on a rich discourse about the neighborhood.
- Seniors may gather regularly in certain coffee shops to talk with each other about what's going on.
- Teens and young adults will do much of their communicating via electronic means, such as text messaging or Facebook. Think about how to access and gather information about the issues and themes that concern these young people.
- People tend to gather at local coffee shops.
- The busiest stores and shops are where you will find a good cross section of the neighborhood.
- There will be certain bus stops where many people wait each morning.
- If there are clubs, gyms, or community centers, you will find people gathered there.

Here are questions to think about as you listen to neighborhood stories:

- What issues and conversations are important to various groups? How are these being expressed? What is behind the emotions of the conversations?
- What are the needs and concerns of various groups?

- Who speaks for the community? Why are they seen as important voices? What are they saying?
- Who doesn't have a voice in this community? Why might this be the case?
- Who are the historians and poets of the community? What are they saying about the neighborhood?
- What resources does the neighborhood have? What is absent and why?
- Who has power? Who is without power? Why?
- What topics of conversation concerning the neighborhood keep coming up?

We've lost the art of talking with one another. In fact sometimes people feel threatened by our questions, thinking we are intruding on their privacy. A person needs to feel safe before he or she will enter into this kind of conversation, so you will need to be sensitive to these feelings and through time and your own willingness to be vulnerable create safe spaces for conversations. Here are some simple questions:

- When did you first move into this neighborhood?
- What brought you here?
- What are your best memories of this neighborhood?
- What do you like best about the area?
- Tell me about your family. Does your extended family live here too?
- What would you love to see happen in this community?

Step 6: Discern What God Is Up To in the Neighborhood

As we listen to stories, we may be able to discern what God is up to in the neighborhood. This is a new way of thinking about God, the gospel, and mission. Sometimes we come to believe the only place where we can really know anything about what God is doing is when we're parked on a pew in a church building, listening to a sermon, or gathered in a small group, reading the Bible with people we've known for a very long time. But what if God wants us to discover the Spirit's working in our very own neighborhoods? What might it mean to have our eyes opened and our minds converted to this idea that God is out there ahead of us in the neighborhood and is doing something? How might we discover this?

In some ways this will feel like the most difficult step to take. You need to practice discernment or the naming of what you believe God might be up to in your neighborhood. This discernment/naming process comes through your dwelling in the Word together and your listening to the stories of the people in the neighborhood. In one sense we are taking this process one step further by asking, In the midst of all we have done, how do we dwell together with God so we can listen to what the Spirit might be saying about God's presence in all this?

Simon Carey Holt in his book *God and Engaging the Neighborhood: Spirituality and Mission in the Neighborhood* writes that this naming is not a solitary business but a communal practice. He wants us to understand something of the journey involved in this way of being a local church.[4] Most of us are schooled in making individual decisions about fairly important things in life. We might talk to others about buying a new house or accepting a job offer, but usually we make private decisions on our own and tell others about them. Often this is a good process, but an unintended consequence may be that we begin to think the most important actions or decisions are the ones we do by ourselves, because we have not included others in them.

We need to develop the practice of discussing decisions with others. This is a little like developing an effective golf swing or mastering a difficult choir number. We must learn some new skills and do them over and over again until they become natural to us. The practice of *naming what God is doing in our neighborhood* is like that; it calls for learning new habits and doing them over and over again until they become a part of who we are. We do it with others, sharing what we are hearing and then discerning together what God may be doing. We will not always get it right but, as we practice together, we will have more and more success in understanding what God is doing. Sometimes we will have little more than an inkling or hunch, but other times we'll see it clearly and have a burning conviction to be involved. This process requires testing out ideas and perceptions, and this is always done more effectively with others rather than alone.

Step 7: Get Involved

To be the church is to be the hands and feet of Jesus. The call to the neighborhood is a call to discover what God is already doing and become a part of it.

In this step the group puts together what it has been discovering. You will need to make a list of places and events where God is working and where you could possibly get involved. Then work out together how you will join in during the coming months. Each time the group meets, report on your experiences and what you're learning together as you continue to dwell in the Word.

Step 8: Report—What Are We Learning?

At this point groups that are becoming involved in a neighborhood should share their experiences with the church (they may not all be ready at the same time). They should also put together a simple report to the church board. This can be done in all kinds of creative ways (for example: take others for a walk through your community, pointing out what you've observed, showing places where you've seen God at work). The purpose is to give the church and its board the information and insight they need to discern how your church can continue this journey of moving back into the neighborhood.

Step 9: Commit—What Do We Do Next?

After groups have shared with the board and the church, the final step is for the leadership to work with the whole church community in naming what it is learning about moving back into the neighborhood and determining the next steps it will take together on this journey.

Notes

Introduction

1. Joshua Cooper Ramos, *The Age of the Unthinkable* (London: Little, Brown, 2009).

2. See Luke 10:1–12.

3. See Alan J. Roxburgh and Fred Romanuk, *The Missional Leader* (San Francisco: Jossey-Bass, 2005); and Alan J. Roxburgh and M. Scott Boren, *Introducing the Missional Church* (Grand Rapids: Baker, 2009).

Chapter 2 A Parable of Three Friends

1. Darrell Guder and Lois Barrett, eds., *Missional Church: A Vision for the Sending of the Church in North America* (Grand Rapids: Eerdmans, 1998).

2. See Geoffrey Wainwright's excellent theological biography *Lesslie Newbigin: A Theological Life* (Oxford: Oxford University Press, 2000); as well as Michael Goheen, *As the Father Has Sent Me, I Am Sending You*, doctoral thesis, 2000; and Paul Weston's excellent Newbigin reader: *Lesslie Newbigin—Missionary Theologian* (Grand Rapids: Eerdmans, 2006).

3. Weston, *Lesslie Newbigin*, 12.

4. Lesslie Newbigin, *The Other Side of 1984: Questions for the Church* (Geneva: World Council of Churches, 1983).

5. Lesslie Newbigin, *The Gospel in a Pluralist Society* (Grand Rapids: Eerdmans, 1989).

6. Lesslie Newbigin, *The Open Secret* (Grand Rapids: Eerdmans, 1978).

7. Lesslie Newbigin, *Foolishness to the Greeks* (Grand Rapids: Eerdmans, 1986).

8. See Mel Lawrence, *The Whole Church* (San Francisco: Jossey-Bass, 2009); Eddie Gibbs, *Church Morph* (Grand Rapids: Baker, 2009); Larry Osborne, *Sticky*

Church (Grand Rapids: Zondervan, 2009); Linda Bergquist and Allen Karr, *Church Turned Inside Out* (San Francisco: Jossey-Bass, 2010).

9. Colin Greene and Martin Robinson, *Metavista: Bible, Church and Mission in an Age of Imagination* (Colorado Springs: Authentic Media, 2008).

Intermezzo The Language House

1. Mark Lau Branson, "Ecclesiology and Leadership for the Missional Church," chapter 4 in *The Missional Church in Context: Helping Congregations Develop Contextual Ministry*, ed. Craig Van Gelder (Grand Rapids: Eerdmans, 2007), 95.

2. For an extremely helpful assessment of what "culture" is about and how we are shaped by narratives and stories that are not always consciously present to us, see James Davison Hunter, *To Change the World: The Irony, Tragedy, and Possibility of Christianity in the Late Modern World* (Oxford: Oxford University Press, 2010).

3. Charles Taylor, *Modern Social Imaginaries* (Durham: Duke University Press, 2004).

4. Ibid., 23.

5. Branson, "Ecclesiology and Leadership," 95.

6. Branson, personal conversation.

7. This is not the only way social imaginaries are formed and extended in a social group. Practices are equally important. The habits we build into our everyday lives also shape the way a social imaginary forms the background narrative of a group. Most of the time, such practices are, again, part of the "taken for granted, this is the way the world works" understanding we have of life. A simple example of such practices illustrates the power of a social imaginary. The automobile is primarily used to enhance the individualistic social imaginary. The evidence is simple to find—drive on a highway that has an HOV lane and note the percentage of people able to use it. In other words, we design institutions and structures (like highways and "single-family" dwellings) that embody this deeper-level social imaginary.

In a church there may be a major value on becoming a "community." In practicing this value people come to church along highways in automobiles that are mostly about individuals getting about; people go to small groups from their single-family dwellings in which everyone has his or her own private, personal space in the form of specialized rooms. Thus we see how the social imaginary is really determining the practices and habits of our everyday lives over against church values, the vision and mission statements people publicly announce.

8. Branson, "Ecclesiology and Leadership," 95.

9. In our home (our language house) we live as an extended family across three generations. This is not just a chance event or just an economic decision but a commitment to a social imaginary that seeks to move away from self-actualized individualism to a commitment of living within a different narrative. This embodies a set of practices informed by a language different from expressive individualism

and single-family dwellings. It refuses to take this language of self as primary or determinative of human thriving.

10. One of the ways to interpret this concept of a language house is to conclude that language is nothing more than a human construct describing and defining the particular way a social group has come to explain, manage, and control the world. In this sense, language is about the way a group has its own "truth"; it is a language-constructed truth that points to nothing beyond or outside itself in the world. Language, in this sense, represents the way groups socially construct reality and nothing more.

This is not what is meant by "language house" in this discussion. While it is the case that every social group can form, extend, and practice its life only through language, this does not mean language is nothing more than group think. As indicated in the previous paragraph, language is also how any social group expresses the ways they are claimed and shaped by that which is greater than themselves. Christians, for example, would claim that their languages of worship and confession are not just socially constructed narratives but the deepest expressions of how they understand the ways God has come to and encounters them in their tradition. Language is also about the ways we give voice to, articulate, put into actual life, and shepherd the world and the gift of God's life that comes to us.

Chapter 4 Finding God in the Concrete

1. See Merold Wesphal, "Against Romantic Hermeneutics: Away from Psychologism," chapter 3 in *Whose Community? Which Interpretation?* (Grand Rapids: Baker, 2009); and Taylor, *Modern Social Imaginaries*.

Chapter 5 Texts That Propose a World

1. See Walter Brueggemann, *Texts under Negotiation* (Philadelphia: Fortress, 1993), chapters 1 and 2; and Greene and Robinson, *Metavista*, 109–11.

2. Peter Martin, *Samuel Johnson: A Biography* (Cambridge, MA: Harvard University Press, 2008).

3. Muriel Barbery, *The Elegance of the Hedgehog* (New York: Europa Editions, 2008).

4. Toby Lester, *The Fourth Part of the World: The Race to the Ends of the Earth and the Epic Story of the Map That Gave America Its Name* (New York: Free Press, 2009).

5. Brueggemann, *Texts under Negotiation*, 17.

6. Ibid., 25.

7. Greene and Robinson, *Metavista*, 109–10. Greene and Robinson offer an important proposal in terms of the multiple narratives (language houses) that characterize our time and how this multiplicity of narratives creates not a singular

world but a *metavista* of stories and language houses. Their important book addresses the question of how we might, again, be drawn into the world of God's particular story in our time.

8. Ibid., 111.

9. You can see this image by simply Googling *The School of Athens*.

10. Charles Lutwidge Dodgson, *Alice's Adventures in Wonderland*.

11. A wide range of literature concerning biblical interpretation has developed around this understanding of Scripture as drama that shapes and calls the community of God's people to embody the drama in their own lives. See Nicholas Lash, *Theology on the Way to Emmaus* (Eugene, OR: Wipf and Stock, 2005); Samuel Wells, *Improvisation: The Drama of Christian Ethics* (Grand Rapids: Brazos, 2004).

Chapter 6 Shifting Worlds

1. See Andrew J. Bacevich, *The Limits of Power: The End of American Exceptionalism* (New York: Metropolitan Books, 2008); and Fareed Zakaria, *The Post American World* (New York: Norton, 2009).

Chapter 7 The Context and Crisis

1. See David Bosch, *Transforming Mission: Paradigm Shifts in the Theology of Mission* (Maryknoll, NY: Orbis, 1991), 84–85.

2. See Joel B. Green, *The Theology of the Gospel of Luke* (Cambridge: Cambridge University Press, 1998), 16–21.

3. Barry Harvey, *Another City: An Ecclesiological Primer for a Post-Christian World* (Harrisburg, PA: Trinity Press, 1999), 21.

4. Green, *Theology of the Gospel of Luke*, 8–9.

5. Bosch, *Transforming Mission*, 85.

Chapter 8 The Boundary-Breaking Spirit

1. Jerusalem at Pentecost would have been filled with these pilgrims from outside of Palestine—the so-called Greek parts of the world. We can assume that a good number of the people drawn into the church after Pentecost were from this group who, parenthetically, would have been older men and women. This is important in terms of understanding the issues that quickly surface in Jerusalem, such as the sharing of goods (these people stayed on and so there were big issues of food and accommodation) and, later, there comes the question of the "Greek" widows.

2. Jehu Hanciles, *Beyond Christendom: Globalization, African Migration, and the Transformation of the West* (Maryknoll, NY: Orbis, 2008), 94.

3. One suspects that letters, such as Ephesians, would by this time have circulated among these late-century Christian communities so that they were familiar with the cosmic dimensions of the incarnation as expressed, for example, in Ephesians 1:9–11.

Chapter 9 The Strange New Ways of God

1. It is often assumed that a certain kind of American exceptionalism made this continent different from Europe in terms of its strength, but as Hanciles argues, the reasons might lie elsewhere. He states, "At the very least, massive Christian immigration throughout the nineteenth century is perhaps the most important single reason why the decline of Christianity in America at the end of the 20th century is less substantial than Europe's—America, as Andrew Walls comments, simply 'started its Christian decline from a much higher base than Europe did'" (*Beyond Christendom*, 7).

2. Some biblical manuscripts have the number seventy-two, which is probably the more accurate translation, but since many popular Bible translations use seventy, that will be used in this section.

3. Bosch, *Transforming Mission*, 85–94.

4. See Alan J. Roxburgh, *Missional Map Making* (San Francisco: Jossey-Bass, 2010).

Chapter 10 A New Set of Practices

1. I am referring to the heirs of the British and European churches formed in the sixteenth-century reformations—these are "Western" churches that assumed power and privilege, whether they were Presbyterian, Baptist, Methodist, Mennonite, Lutheran, or all those new forms of evangelicalism that emerged later in modernity reacting against Anglicanism or other forms of dominant Anglo-European Protantism.

2. In our culture the language of "stranger" has received a diabolical reversal of meaning. Walk through neighborhoods these days, and the signs indicate that strangers are not welcomed but feared. Strangers are reported to the police. In the time of Luke the stranger was welcomed, received, housed, and fed. The core reason for the curse that is called down on some of these towns and villages was that they failed utterly to offer hospitality to the stranger. By that accounting, most housing developments today, filled with middle-class Christians, seem to have come to a place where they are fundamentally incapable of receiving and welcoming the stranger.

3. Alexander Schmemann, *For the Life of the World: Sacraments and Orthodoxy* (New York: St. Vladimir Seminary Press, 1988), 5.

4. This statement, as indicated throughout this book, does not mean there is no place for the traditions and liturgical life of churches as they worship God and shape discipleship through catechesis. As I have said over and over again, this is not what is at stake here. The issue is the ongoing ecclesiocentric nature of almost all our church life and the call to reimagine the location where we will discern how the boundary-breaking Spirit is reshaping and re-forming God's future in the West.

Chapter 11 Peace, Healing, and the Kingdom of God

1. Each question seeks to deny the materiality of Jesus and/or God's work in the world. Each seeks to "spiritualize" the Christian life as if the ordinary and material have no importance to the way of the gospel. As such, there is this strange, unreal belief that someone's daily life can be radically separated from their experience with God, so sitting at a table with another is just that and no more. This is the deep suspicion Gnostic Christians bring to this conversation. They seem unable to see that when we are formed in the material practices of Christian life (prayer, Eucharist, daily office, and so on), we are embodying a narrative that shapes us materially as God's people. It is the inability to conceive of this reality that makes them conclude that this kind of entering and dwelling at the table of the other will result only in "community development" or "social work" or just good feelings among people. This is a poverty of Christian imagination as well as a sign of the utter absence of any real catechesis and formation within our church communities.

2. See Stephen's speech before he is stoned to death in Acts 7.

Chapter 12 Rules for Radicals

1. See Roxburgh and Romanuk, *The Missional Leader.*

2. See Alan Roxburgh, *The Sky Is Falling: Leaders Lost in Transition* (Eagle, ID: Allelon Publishing, 2006).

3. See Roxburgh, *Missional Map Making.*

Chapter 13 Beginning the Journey

1. Alan Roxburgh, *Reaching a New Generation* (Downers Grove, IL: InterVarsity, 1993), 105.

2. *Moving Back into the Neighborhood* is a comprehensive workbook, available at http://roxburghmissionalnet.com.

3. These groups need to be formed among people who live near one another. Usually there are groups of people in the church living fairly close together. When one group of churches realized that, as individual churches, they did not have many people living near each other, they began to problem solve for themselves in a wonderful way. By looking at the places where people lived from among their various churches, they discovered there were lots of people living close to one another, so they formed cross-church groups in local neighborhoods. The Spirit calls us to risk and experiment with our imaginations about what is possible.

4. Simon Carey Holt, *God and Engaging the Neighborhood: Spirituality and Mission in the Neighborhood* (Brunswick: Acorn Press, 2007).

Alan Roxburgh is president of Roxburgh Missional Network, an international group of practitioners and academics committed to partnering with and calling forth missional churches and mission-shaped leaders. Alan served as a pastor for more than twenty-five years. He is an author, teacher, conference speaker, and consultant to churches and denominational systems around the world. His books include *Reaching a New Generation: Strategies for Tomorrow's Church; The Missionary Congregation, Leadership, and Liminality; Crossing the Bridge: Leadership in a Time of Change; The Sky Is Falling: Leaders Lost in Transition; Introducing the Missional Church: What It Is, Why It Matters, How to Become One;* and *The Missional Leader: Equipping Church to Reach a Changing World.* He was also a member of the writing team that authored *Missional Church: A Vision for the Sending of the Church in North America.*

Alan leads conferences and seminars with denominations, congregations, and seminaries across North America, Europe, Asia, Australia, New Zealand, and the UK, as well as consulting with these groups in the areas of leadership development and systems change for missional transformation.

When not traveling or writing, Alan enjoys mountain biking, hiking, cooking, and hanging out with his wife, Jane, and their five grandchildren as well as drinking great coffee in the Pacific Northwest.

An Accessible Introduction to the Missional Church Movement

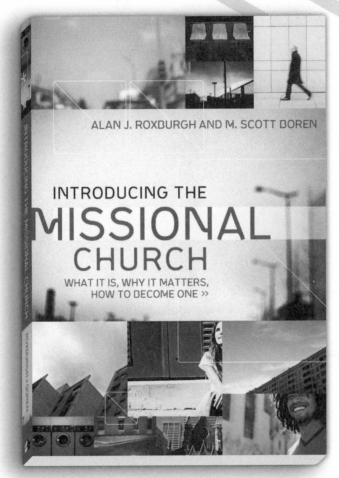

9780801072123

Ours is a post-Christian culture, making it necessary for church leaders to think like missionaries right here at home. In *Introducing the Missional Church*, two leading voices in the missional movement provide an accessible introduction, explaining how the movement developed, why it's important, and how churches can become more missional.

BakerBooks
a division of Baker Publishing Group
www.BakerBooks.com